MOVEMENT EDUCATION: THEORY and PRACTICE

MARIANNE FROSTIG, Ph.D.

In Association with PHYLLIS MASLOW, M.A.

FOLLETT PUBLISHING COMPANY/CHICAGO

Acknowledgments

This book, as does every human enterprise, represents the collaborative efforts of many people.

The children and the teachers of The Marianne Frostig Center of Educational Therapy have contributed their knowledge, their enthusiasm, and their creativity to this book. They have tried out the ideas and performed the exercises and given us their spontaneous and their reasoned feedback. Mr. Thomas Huestis, supervisor of the movement education program at the Center, has been especially helpful.

Very special thanks and appreciation are due Dr. Bryant Cratty, Professor of Physical Education and Director of the Perceptual-Motor Laboratory, UCLA, who wrote the Foreword and read the rough draft of the manuscript; to Dr. L. Lavonne Stock, Professor of Physical Education, California State College at Long Beach, who also read the manuscript; to Leon Whitsell, M.D., who read Chapter 4; to Dr. Juana de Laban, Professor of Dance, UCLA, who read Chapter 5; and to George Robson, Welty School of Educational Therapy, Glendale, California, who read Chapter 8. Their suggestions and comments have helped clarify our ideas and have added many valuable contributions. We fully acknowledge our own responsibility for whatever errors of omission and commission may still remain.

Anyone who writes a book becomes aware of the inestimable value of a capable, dedicated, intelligent secretary. Over the past decade Mrs. Phyllis Gedge has demonstrated these qualities, and she has been a most valued assistant in the preparation of the manuscript. Miss Donna Joseph and Miss Joan Crown have also capably assisted in its preparation.

Mr. David Horne has given us much help in the preliminary editing. The main editorial work has been the responsibility of Miss Jean Adams, Senior Editor, Follett Educational Corporation. Her outstanding editorial abilities, her keen understanding, and her patience have been instrumental in bringing this book to publication. She indeed has performed many tasks above and beyond those expected of an editor, and we would like to take this opportunity to express our sincere appreciation to our friend and colleague.

Marianne Frostig, Ph.D.
Phyllis Maslow, M.A.

Foreword

It may prove disquieting for some physical educators to read a text in which physical education is discussed by an educational psychologist. But it is my belief that this book comprises one of the best current references for elucidating and justifying the manner in which movement skills contribute to the total emotional, intellectual, and social development of the growing child.

Special educators and classroom teachers of normal children will benefit from the easy-to-follow games and exercises described in this book. Both graduate and undergraduate students will appreciate the well-documented theory based upon current research and clinical experience.

Dr. Frostig, from her wide background in classroom teaching, psychology, and special education, has brought together descriptions of games and movement activities that she has used with normal children and with children with learning disabilities. The purpose is to promote not only motor skills for their own sake, but also to help develop body awareness, perceptual skills, language, arithmetic concepts, and other academic learnings.

The author does more than simply describe games and activities, however. This text contains material summarizing current research on the nature of motor activities, the manner in which motor activities integrate with other activities, which clinical practices are useful with children who have neurological deficits, as well as current educational methodologies.

Material is presented that dispels some of the prevalent misconceptions surrounding perceptual-motor functions. For example, Dr. Frostig questions the importance attached by some to crossed dominance as an educational handicap for children, citing research findings that indicate that crossed dominance is the rule rather than the exception. At the same time, she is careful to point out the problems that need to be researched.

Dr. Frostig discusses the theories of Kephart, Barsch, and others, and she describes their implications for the classroom teacher. Her language is clear and the thoughts expressed are profound.

A comprehensive picture is presented by the author. Motor performance is depicted in its many faceted complexity, while perceptual attributes are described, as are various cognitive functions, such as categorization, synthesis of information, and response generalization. More important, Dr. Frostig outlines helpful ways in which specific movement skills aid in the development of well defined perceptual and cognitive attributes, a much more welcome procedure than simply presenting a romanticized perceptual-motor novel, which is sometimes seen in current material on the subject. Dr. Frostig does not become evangelical but remains helpfully pragmatic in her approach.

Reading between the lines, one assumes that the author has had formal training as a physical educator, as indeed she has. She studied for two years at the college in Hellerau-Laxenburg, near Vienna, a school training teachers and dancers, where she specialized in movement education for children. Following this training, Dr. Frostig was granted a certificate as a physical education teacher by the city of Vienna. Subsequently she used this training in working with physically and emotionally handicapped children. Her first published paper in the United States, written in 1946, was titled "Motion and Emotion."

During the past eight years, in which I have worked closely with Dr. Frostig in Los Angeles, we have had many of the same children in our respective programs. I am not surprised, therefore, to find that we are in close agreement in our approach to the role of movement skills in education. Unlike some theoreticians, we feel that motor activities have an important, but not preeminent, part to play in the educational process. Movement skills, Dr. Frostig seems to suggest, are important educational tools, not the bases from which the total personality springs.

It is with the vivid elucidation of these tools that Dr. Frostig concerns herself in this text. I am sure the ideas, activities, and theories contained in it will provide for teachers a meaningful and scholarly course within the sometimes ambiguous perceptual-motor labyrinth.

Bryant J. Cratty
University of California at Los Angeles

Contents

Introduction

This book presents a program for teaching movement skills and developing creative movement to enhance the total development of young children — their physical and their psychological abilities, their ability to learn, their ability to get along with one another, their feelings about themselves, and their relationship to the environment.

The exercises and their variations and the procedures to develop movement skills, creativity, body awareness, and other abilities are but the practical application of the basic postulates and theoretical considerations of learning through movement. The theories discussed in this textbook are related to the teacher's everyday work with children on the playground, in the gymnasium, and in the classroom. Knowledge of the theories permits adaptation of the program to satisfy the children's individual needs and enables the teacher to enlarge, enrich, and develop the movement repertoire of the children, as well as her own skill in developing their repertoire. The teacher will learn how to use movement for the promotion of academic skills and to correctly appraise its value and limitations in relation to academics.

This is not a physical education program in the traditional meaning of the term — development and care of the body, hygiene, systematic exercises, and sports and games. The goals of this program are more global. To achieve these goals, the teacher must not regard her job as a mechanical one. To be most effective, she must know the goals toward which she is working in movement education, and she must base her choice of exercises and activities on what is known about children's needs and children's growth. She must adapt this program to her particular situation, and in doing so consider all aspects of human development.

Application of educational methods without understanding the basic assumptions on which they are based often leads to distortion of methods. Montessori, for example, warned against restricting the inventiveness of children and teachers. Nevertheless, some schools purporting to use Montessori methods today have replaced her creative, flexible approach with regimentation.

Essential and basic insights into educational processes set forth by the great educators of the past — from Socrates (whose methods are now being revived and used in the "discovery" method) through Locke, Rousseau, Montessori, Dewey, and the scholars of our time — are all too often forgotten as fads and new directions in education spring up.

Learning theorists, such as Skinner, have emphasized the need to begin where a child is, to progress in a careful step-by-step manner, to provide immediate feedback, and to ensure success for every child. These principles are valid, but other equally valid principles need to be emphasized: the need to provide opportunities for discovery and inventiveness (Bruner); to take into account the special needs of young children (Rousseau); to consider children's interests (Dewey); to adapt content and methods to the stages of children's development (so masterfully described by Piaget); and to integrate and to structure across content areas (Bruner).

Our intent in this book is four-fold.

First, it is to arouse the teacher's interest in and awareness of the multifaceted theoretical foundations of the methods she uses and to help her make a critical evaluation of theories concerning physical education and of practices recommended by others so that she may choose wisely.

Second, it is to emphasize children's emotional needs. Development of joy of living is an important goal of education. But that goal is frequently called unscientific (feelings are not measurable) or unimportant and unworthy of discussion.

The concept that emotional development is a necessary consideration of education is often eliminated from serious educational discussion. The behavior of people, animals, and machines is considered equivalent. But children, unlike machines, do not usually break down immediately if they are mistreated. The effects of miseducation may become apparent only when they reach adulthood.

Pressuring, overloading with facts, placing limits on high spirits and creativity, and robbing children of pleasure may, indeed, lead to a world devoid of joy and filled with anxiety and hatred — a world increasingly bent on self-destruction.

Third, our intent is to help the teacher use methods that will make the children eager to be in school and eager to learn; methods that will make the teacher eager to teach. The school not only puts repressive pressures on children; it puts them on teachers. The children react to pressures by developing behavior problems, to which the teacher, in desperation, responds with additional repressive measures. Thus the atmosphere of pleasure and eagerness so essential to learning is eroded.

Fourth, our intent is to be comprehensive and practical — to give not only theory but to suggest methods designed to help overcome some of the difficulties inherent in our educational system (such as the long hours children are required to sit still) as well as the learning difficulties inherent in some children (such as those caused by hyperactivity). Furthermore, the program is written and structured so that the classroom teacher can conduct movement education, as well as the physical education teacher.

The format of the program is also practical. In addition to this textbook, which covers all facets of the program, there is available a set of cards, each card with one exercise and variations printed on it, and a teacher's guide to facilitate management of the movement education program for the busy teacher.

The program is planned for children from kindergarten through the primary grades, but many parts of it can also be used in higher grades if more structured games and sports, training in endurance, and more training in speed are added.

Studies of urban living show that it is an added but unavoidable responsibility of the school to help counteract the destructive effects of urban living and to help children recover from unhappy experiences caused by the unrest, the anxiety, and the adverse conditions of their lives. Self-awareness, creativity, and the ability to learn can be promoted by movement education, and thus a child's self-concept and his feelings and behavior can be favorably influenced.

We hope that physical education teachers, classroom teachers, and students in teacher training will get practical, measurable help from this book so that they and the children will experience the joys of discovery and mastery and the social and emotional satisfactions that are the results of successful working and living with a group.

This youngster is proud that he can jump over the dowel in midair while holding it with both hands.

Chapter I

Learning Through Movement

The central goals of movement education are the promotion of good health and a sense of well-being and the development of sensory-motor skills and of self-awareness.

A well administered movement education program — one that is integrated with all subjects in the school curriculum (Fleming, 1968) — can achieve much more. A child's physical fitness and the quality of his movements influence (and in turn are influenced by) all of his psychological abilities — his abilities to communicate, to perceive, and to solve problems — and the way he feels and interacts with others. Such a program can also help to enhance the creativity of children and even to improve their ability to learn academic skills. Basic characteristics of a child — for instance, the speed of response, the ability to focus attention, and the ability to exert control — can be enhanced. And children's awareness of their environment and of time and space dimensions of all experiences can be sharpened.

Health and a Sense of Well-Being

A child's growth pattern, blood circulation, and resistance to disease are positively influenced by physical activity. A child's natural joy in movement and his feelings of mastery as he progresses in learning movement skills enhance his emotional health. Better physical and emotional health in turn have implications for a child's ability to concentrate on tasks and to learn.

Children are often severely restricted in their physical activities. Those who live in cities, and even those who live in suburbs, lack space for free movement and for self-initiated games (Hanson, 1968). With the growth of automation and the ubiquitous use of mechanical locomotion, physical effort is disappearing from the lives of most people of all ages, with the result that muscular and circulatory weaknesses are prevalent. Planned physical activities are therefore necessary for all age groups.

Among the most frequent health hazards are incorrect posture and incorrect movements. Williams and Worthingham (1957) state that 30 percent of more than 5,000 patients referred to a clinic for physical therapy had back disabilities and that 70 percent of this group suffered from lower back strain. Training that corrects posture and movement that strengthens back muscles could eliminate the majority of these muscular difficulties.

Movement Skills

Some critics of physical education argue that physical skills are unnecessary in everyday life and that teaching such skills is therefore of limited value. Even granting the incorrect and narrow assumption that teaching movement skills is the only goal of movement education, movement education can help us become more effective in everyday life.

Most of us are unaware that everyday activities, such as walking, climbing stairs, and stooping, involve complex movements that are often poorly executed, leading to inefficiency in daily tasks and sometimes to injury. Movement skills are therefore a necessary part of fitness, by which is meant the possession of health, vigor, and the ability to perform efficiently everyday tasks.

We do not mean by fitness the attainment of the maximum in physical prowess and endurance (Cureton, 1965). The production of a population of skilled athletes should not be a major goal of movement education in school. To quote Weiss (1964), "It is more important to develop the habit of being physically active than to develop high levels of physical fitness." Nevertheless, movement skills are necessary for sports, for group and individual recreational activities, and for creative movement, all of which contribute to good physical and mental health.

Sensory-Motor Skills

Improvement of movement skills is important, but movement does not exist in isolation. It is accompanied by sensations and perceptual experiences.

Movement is often initiated by perceptions, but it is always guided by kinesthetic and other sensory stimuli, which make possible the successful completion of a movement sequence.

Movement can, of course, be elicited by thought, as when we decide to take a book from a shelf, write a letter, go shopping, or visit a friend. And generally we are more aware of the role of our thoughts and plans than we are of the role of sensory stimuli in originating and guiding movements. Thus we are prone to underestimate or ignore the sensory side of sensory-motor tasks. We are usually aware, for example, that our decision to make a cup of tea initiates a ritual culminating in bringing a brimming cup to our lips. But we are probably not conscious of our eyes guiding our hands in turning on the water faucet, filling the tea kettle, and turning on the stove, of our ears informing us that the water is boiling, or of our kinesthetic sense informing us of the correctness of each movement, thus initiating and continuing the movement sequence.

Conscious movement is therefore best understood as a sensory-motor activity, and it should be considered, trained, and evaluated in both its aspects — the sensory and the motor. The teacher, therefore, should not be interested in movement alone. She should also be concerned with the initiation and direction of movement by auditory, visual, tactile, and kinesthetic stimuli.

Self-Awareness

Awareness of self and of the ability to change and to master the body and many aspects of the environment is established to a high degree during the first twelve to twenty-four months of life. But some children, and even adults, lack this awareness or it is distorted.

Mechanization of education and the pressure in school to master an ever-increasing mass of facts and skills lead to neglect of subject matter that develops awareness of self and awareness of others. Environments that lack space for individual pursuits also lead to loss of self-awareness. This loss is felt as lack of identity, so often bemoaned.

Today our schools are crowded with children who lack self-awareness and self-acceptance. The warmth that teachers can give such children is sorely needed by them: They are often humiliated and hopeless because the adults they know are unfriendly, since they too are anxious, harassed, and angry. Teachers can help children replace resentment and anger with friendliness, helpfulness, and love for others. They can help to fill with light and joy lives that often have known misery and despair.

Fortunately, movement education can help children gain self-awareness and prepare them to withstand the pressures and anxieties of their lives as children and as adults. Movement education in all its forms promotes awareness of oneself, and work in pairs and in groups helps children become more aware of each other and teaches them to work together to achieve common goals. Chapters 4, 5, and 9 contain many suggestions to enhance children's social adjustment and emotional development.

Time and Space Awareness

Awareness of the world around us depends on awareness of time and space because all objects and all events occur in time and space.

The infant lives in the here and now. Past and future are beyond his scope, glimpsed only at odd moments. Space is limited by what is within his immediate reach, expanding to a broader environment only as he masters locomotion.

In movement education, concepts of time and space are not only experienced directly, but they coalesce in the movement. Without such time and space awareness, perception of the world is blurred, permitting only a narrow range of experiences. If the world of a school child is to be clarified, it must transcend his own body (he as a person), his home, even his community, and it has to encompass the past — the time before he was — as well as the future, which exists in his plans, dreams, and hopes. Time and space awareness are poorly developed in many school children. In some, as in infants, time and space are restricted to the here and now. These children cannot postpone pleasure regardless of adverse results; only their own immediate needs are perceived. Asocial or antisocial behavior is frequently the result.

Improvement of Global Functions

Retardation of certain developmental functions, including loss of self-awareness and the awareness of the environment, may occur because of environmental deprivation, because of a defect in the regulatory functions of the nervous system, or because of both. Lack of awareness may be an isolated symptom or part of a syndrome that is well known to the teacher of the culturally deprived or of the neurologically handicapped.

John (1967) states that damage to the nervous system may disturb all regulatory functions, impairing motivation, short-term memory, and orientation; creating disinhibition; interfering with the establishment and maintenance of a set in responding; and increasing distractibility. All aspects of behavior are then affected.

The teacher who works with children with learning difficulties or with inner city children knows their frequent inability to direct their attention and to select relevant stimuli. She realizes that these children need to be strongly motivated to work and helped to find the energy to overcome difficulties. She is acquainted with their inability to remember what they have just heard, and she knows how often they forget what they seemed to know so well the day before. But it is often hard for her not to be annoyed by their difficulty in maintaining attention and by their disorganization and impulsivity.

Movement education has often been suggested as a remedy when the regulatory functions of the nervous system are defective. We agree with this assumption. The irritability, hyperactivity, and impulsivity of neurologically handicapped children can be ameliorated through movement education. We discuss in Chapter 9 specific ways in which movement education may be used to ameliorate behavioral disturbances. Certain principles of teaching need to be followed for adequate results with all children.

Teaching Principles

1. The atmosphere should be one of joy and spontaneity. The success of the program depends in large part on the satisfaction of the teacher and on the increasing enjoyment of the children.

2. Children should be made aware that their pleasure and spontaneity can be maintained only if there is order and control. They should be prepared to take increasing responsibility for their own control. Most children become aware early in life that control of movement is essential if they are not to fall and to bump themselves, and eventually they can learn that such control is necessary for all activities.

3. Each movement education lesson should include exercises that train the attributes of movement and exercises that help children to be creative.

4. Specific exercises, such as those to help children learn a movement sequence, to recognize shapes, or to follow written directions, need not be included in every lesson. They should be used only when it is desirable to integrate such specific objectives into the curriculum for a particular child, group, or class.

5. The teacher must understand the principles on which the exercises are based and use the exercises accordingly. Most exercises can be performed in a variety of ways, depending on the abilities of the children, on their interests, on the goals set for an individual child, and on the requirements of the total curriculum. (See Chapter 9 for examples.)

6. It is of utmost importance to give children success experiences and to avoid having them fail. Some children show severe difficulties in movement skills. These children may feel inadequate and helpless to do an exercise if the teacher's instructions are inflexible. John may be able to throw and catch a beanbag while skipping; Billy may have to stand still to be successful.

The teacher also may often have to begin by teaching the simplest positions and movements, such as stretching the arms upward or jumping or standing with feet apart. This is true for some very young children and for many children with learning difficulties.

7. Finally, the teacher must be guided by the children's reactions to the exercises. She must observe when help is needed, when simpler exercises have to be used, when a change of tempo is indicated, or when greater challenges would be of advantage. She must be flexible in her planning.

Works Cited

Cureton, T. K. *Physical Fitness and Dynamic Health.* New York: Dial Press, 1965.

Fleming, R. S. Movement — An essential in a good school day. In *Physical Education for Children's Healthful Living.* Washington, D. C.: Bulletin No. 23-A, Association for Childhood Education International, 1968, 13-20.

Hanson, M. R. The new look in elementary school physical education. In *Physical Education for Children's Healthful Living.* Washington, D. C.: Bulletin 23-A, Association for Childhood Education International, 1968, 71-76.

John, E. R. *Mechanisms of Memory.* New York: Academic Press, 1967.

Weiss, R. A. Is physical fitness our most important objective? *Journal of Health, Physical Education, Recreation,* 1964, **35**, 1-7.

Williams, M., and Worthingham, C. *Therapeutic Exercise.* Philadelphia: Saunders, 1957.

Chapter 2

The Developmental Sequence

Longitudinal studies of children show that certain abilities develop in a definite sequence. A child usually learns to walk before he learns to talk in sentences. He learns to grasp objects, such as blocks, and to put them on top of each other long before he masters tools and implements, such as pencils, crayons, and scissors. He learns to talk before he learns to read and to scribble before he learns to write.

An equally important observation is that certain ways of communicating with and mastering the environment develop at a maximum rate during certain age spans or developmental phases. It is important for the teacher to know when certain abilities should develop in young children and the sequence in which they unfold so that she can choose the most appropriate curriculum and teaching methods.

Development follows a definite sequence and this sequence is fixed. This has been found to be true regardless of which aspect of development is studied. Freud (1938, 1949), who explored the child's emotional development (psychosexual characteristics); Erikson (1968), who studied the interrelationships of the child's social and emotional development; Piaget (1966, 1967), Bruner (1956, 1966), and others, who focused on cognitive development; McCarthy (1954), Vygotsky (1965), and others who were concerned with language — all of these scholars reported that they found predictable changes in the psychological functions of the growing child.

The names of the phases and their descriptions vary somewhat from scholar to scholar, but in general their findings and descriptions agree.

Abilities that Develop During the Sensory-Motor Phase

The first phase in a child's life is the sensory-motor phase. By sensory-motor functions is meant the child's mode of exploration of himself and of the world around him through a simultaneous use of his sense modalities and movements. Sensory-motor functions develop maximally during the first eighteen to twenty-four months of a child's life.

An infant learns to recognize his mother by touch as well as by sight. He is likely to play with his blanket with his hands and suck and kick it, all at the same time. A baby playing with toys will typically touch, throw, and lick them, hide and retrieve them, push, pull, and

23

shake them, listen to the sounds as he bangs them around, and at the same time watch what happens to the toys. He thus becomes cognizant of the outer world and learns to achieve some mastery over it by multiple sensory-motor means.

Four distinct groups of skills develop during the sensory-motor phase: (1) The infant learns to recognize many features of his environment. (2) He becomes aware of himself as distinct from his environment. (3) He learns to change his body position (lying to sitting; standing to kneeling) and also to move in space (crawl, walk, run). (4) He learns to grasp, hold, release, and manipulate objects at will.

The mastery of these four sensory-motor skills constitutes the child's first steps toward independence, ability to adjust to the demands of the environment, and toward future learning. Training in sensory-motor abilities is therefore a most important aspect of education. If a child lacks any of these abilities, he is handicapped in receiving information and in communicating with his environment. Thus his general development is delayed. All children need training in sensory-motor functions. And many school children are deficient in the abilities they should have acquired during the sensory-motor phase. For such children, training must be thorough and intensive. Movement education can be most effective in developing many sensory-motor skills.

Training in Sensory-Motor Skills

Because of the importance of the sensory-motor phase, training in the four major developmental skills should be included in the school movement education program. As mentioned before, these are the child's awareness of the world around him, the child's awareness of his own body, movement in space, and manipulation (movement of other objects).

For sensory-motor training to be comprehensive, however, other activities besides physical exercises have to be included, mainly manipulative and construction activities — arts and crafts, shopwork, exercises in sensory discrimination (such as with forms, colors, and sizes).

Language

The first developmental phase, the sensory-motor phase, overlaps with and is followed by the period of maximum development of language. The child learns to understand and to use speech. As he learns to communicate through language, he learns about things that are not present, and his awareness begins to include the events of his past and his expectancies of the future. This period of maximum language development lasts until the child is about three or four years old.

Language is deficient in many school-age children. Numerous articles, pamphlets, monographs, and books have been written about the need of culturally deprived children for intensive training in language skills. Minor communication disorders are found in children in every grade. But even more children who develop their language skills at a slower rate than average and have difficulties with expression and understanding language are found in kindergarten and the early primary grades.

Movement education promotes language in the "normal" child as well as in the child with learning difficulties, the culturally deprived child, the child with specific language deficiencies, and the neurologically handicapped child.

How language can be developed in the framework of movement education is discussed in Chapter 6.

Perception

Maximum development of perceptual abilities takes place between the ages of approximately three and one-half to seven years. Various psychologists have used different names for this period. Bruner (1966) calls it the iconic phase. Piaget (1966) refers to the period from the end of the sensory-motor phase (approximately two years) to the beginning of the operational phase (approximately seven years) as pre-operational. He calls perception the intuitive aspect of intelligence and the period in which it predominates the representational phase (approximately four and one-half to seven years).

All of these terms point to the new mode in which the child tries to understand the world around him. The child's experiences have accumulated during the past so that much of what he hears and sees can be perceived immediately by an unconscious comparison with the memories of previous experiences, with the "pictures" (icons) he has stored in his mind. Thus he now understands the world around him mainly with the help of his distance receptors (eyes, ears), and he no longer needs to touch, handle, taste, or smell to recognize objects. How perceptual abilities, which develop subsequent to the period of maximum language development, can be enhanced is discussed in Chapter 6.

Higher Cognitive Functions

Piaget (1966) terms the periods during which higher cognitive functions develop maximally the operational stages; he differentiates between the stage of concrete operations (approximately six and one-half or seven and one-half to eleven years of age) and the stage of formal operations that follows. During the stage of concrete operations the child begins to rely less on perceptions and more on thought processes, although he does not reach the level of abstract thinking he reaches during the stage of formal operations. The physical manipulation by the infant, the later exploration through language (mainly through asking numerous "Why" questions), the exploration through looking and listening (perception) are followed by exploration of the environment through thought.

Movement education can be used by the teacher to directly develop higher thought processes. Chapters 5 and 6 help guide the teacher toward this goal.

Emotional Development and Social Adjustment

In discussing the developmental sequence and its implications for movement education, two other aspects of a child's development need to be mentioned — emotional development and social adjustment.

In contrast to movement, language, perception, and thought processes, neither emotional development nor social adjustment shows one single peak of maximum development, but rather a series of transformations throughout life. Emotional and social development permit the human being to adjust to the demands that different social roles impose at each new age level.

Movement education can help a child to adjust socially and emotionally because it can provide him with successful experiences and permit interrelationships with other children in groups and with a partner. Movement education requires that a child be aware of others in games in which he shares space during physical activities; he has to take turns and to cooperate. He thus develops social awareness and achieves satisfaction through peer relationships and group play. He learns to assume social roles as a leader and as a peer. As a consequence, he is better able to assist and to adjust to others and to new situations.

The emotional development of the child is also furthered through physical exercise. Movement is one of his most important needs. He can express his feelings in movement sequences, and he gains satisfaction in achievement and in social relationships. This topic is discussed further in Chapter 5.

Works Cited

Bruner, J. S. *Toward a Theory of Instruction.* Cambridge, Mass.: Harvard Univ. Press, 1966.

Bruner, J. S., Goodnow, J. J., and Austin, G. A. *A Study of Thinking.* Science Edition. New York: John Wiley, 1956.

Erikson, E. H. *Childhood and Society.* (Rev. ed.) New York: W. W. Norton, 1968. (First published 1950.)

Freud, S. *An Outline of Psychoanalysis.* New York: W. W. Norton, 1949.

Freud, S. Three contributions to the theory of sex. In A. A. Brill (Ed.), *The Basic Writings of Sigmund Freud.* New York: Modern Library, 1938. (First published 1905.)

McCarthy, D. Language development in children. In L. Carmichael (Ed.), *Manual of Child Psychology.* (2nd ed.) New York: John Wiley, 1954. (First published 1946.)

Piaget, J. *Psychology of Intelligence.* Totona, N. J.: Littlefield, Adams, 1966. (First published in French, 1947.)

Piaget, J. *Six Psychological Studies.* New York: Random House, 1967.

Vygotsky, L. S. *Thought and Language.* Cambridge, Mass.: M.I.T. Press, 1965.

Chapter 3

The Attributes of Movement

The objectives of movement education are numerous, and neither theoreticians nor teachers of physical education can agree entirely upon these objectives or their relative importance. But despite the diversity of curricula and methods, every educator would probably agree that the development of movement skills is always a central objective of physical education. For example, Laban (1968) and his followers emphasize mastery of the body during free movement in space (agility, flexibility, and coordination). Kephart (1960) and Godfrey and Kephart (1969) emphasize the mastery of the body in tasks requiring balance and visual skills to achieve transfer of skills to different movement sequences (movement generalizations). In sports, the sprinter tries to promote the attribute of speed; the weight lifter, strength; and the hiker, endurance. But no physical skill, whether needed in dance or sports or gymnastics, is used alone and independent of other physical skills. Thus the harmonious development of physical abilities requires their equal consideration.

Programs Compared

Motor skills are also referred to as the attributes of movement. Through a statistical method called factor analysis, these skills have been analyzed into their components. Nicks and Fleishman (1960) have this to say about factor analysis:

"A direct approach to this problem is a correlational approach in which large numbers of tests are given the same subjects. The assumption is that the tests which correlate with each other measure the same factors, and tests which are uncorrelated measure different factors. The mathematical technique of factor analysis . . . is applied to the correlations to isolate the common factors and to assist in their description and interpretation."*

Various factor analytic studies of movement agree quite well on the different motor abilities that can be isolated. These abilities often show very low correlations among themselves, as, for instance, man-

*Used by permission of the authors.

ual dexterity and general muscular strength. This fact is borne out by observation and is common knowledge. We would not expect the ability to cut diamonds or to pick locks to be necessarily accompanied by prowess on the parallel bars or in weight lifting.

Because of the variety of skills that are thus shown to be involved in movement, there are considerable variations in the movement patterns of children who show sensory-motor disabilities. Some children are relatively proficient in attributes of movement in which others are deficient. When working with children with movement deficits, it is of advantage to analyze carefully the performance of each child and establish his proficiency in each attribute of movement in comparison with his classmates before a movement education program is planned and put into effect. A teacher who is aware of the attributes of movement can observe and evaluate deficiencies in many children.

The table, pages 32-33, compares the results of factor analytic studies of movement with three physical education programs. Nicks and Fleishman (1960) summarized the results of seventy-eight studies. It appears from their review that the majority of studies agree on seven broad areas of physical skills that can be differentiated through factor analysis. They are coordination (including rhythm), flexibility, speed, agility, strength, balance, and endurance. Guilford's earlier factor analytic study of movement skills (1958) is also summarized in the table. His results were in general the same as those reported in later studies. Guilford also introduced another dimension in his analysis — namely the body parts and muscle groups to which the attributes refer. This was done because proficiency in an attribute may not apply to the entire body structure. For example, speed of movement in the fingers is not necessarily accompanied by speed in running. Strength in the arms, which is necessary for performance on the parallel bars, is not always accompanied by strength in the leg muscles, as found in a sprinter.

This second dimension of Guilford's analysis is mentioned to emphasize the necessity for conducting movement education programs that include exercises involving each muscle group in the body that is involved in skeletal movement. By using a variety of positions during the exercises, the beginning teacher can avoid overemphasis on use of the leg muscles at the cost of other muscle groups. If exercises are done lying prone and supine, sitting, kneeling, crouching on all fours, in an upright position, and so on, the body is supported by different muscle groups, and different muscle groups will be involved in movements. (See Chapters 11 and 12 for further steps in assuring a well balanced program of movement education.)

The table compares attributes of movement that are specifically considered in three physical education programs. Some educators emphasize certain movement skills more than others. A critical evaluation of any new physical education program should include an analysis of the program in regard to the movement skills that it tries to improve.

This program and Mosston's program (1966) are among those that try to develop movement skills while taking into account other aspects of children's development, such as language, perceptual and cognitive functions, and emotional and social development.

Mosston, however, is not concerned with integration of movement education in the total school program or in teaching academic skills through movement education. His emphasis is always on the teaching of movement skills, although he is also concerned with the development of social, emotional, and cognitive functions. He requires the pupils to work cooperatively; and he calls for the imagination and inventiveness of both pupils and teachers. His program deserves careful study by the teacher of movement education.

In the physical education program included in *The Slow Learner in the Classroom,* Kephart (1960) includes perceptual, ocular, and memory skills. He specifically mentions gross motor coordination, eye-hand coordination, temporal-spatial translations, posture, laterality, directionality, body image, perceptual processes (mainly form perception and space discrimination), and agility, which he terms flexibility. His program (Kephart, 1960; Godfrey and Kephart, 1969) includes many excellent suggestions.

Other widely known programs focusing on children with learning disabilities are those by Getman (1962) and by Barsch (1965). Both have many valuable suggestions. Another program worth studying is the "Segmented Demonstration Physical Education Program of the Sonoma County (California) Schools" (1969). This all-inclusive program discusses many aspects of physical education, including structured calisthenics and movement exploration.

Some public school programs that have as their explicit goal the development of physical skills do not consider all of the attributes of movement. For instance, the physical education guide for the elementary schools in Los Angeles (1957) mentions specifically only coordination, strength, and agility. Nevertheless, the great variety of exercises in that program ensures that other abilities receive attention also.

Of at least equal importance for the teacher is the knowledge of the different aspects of creative movement (movement exploration), which is discussed in Chapter 5.

Factors in Human Movement and Physical Education Programs, by Authors

Attributes of Movement	Guilford[1]	Nicks and Fleishman[2] (Summary of 78 Studies)	Mosston[3]	Kephart[4]	Frostig and Maslow
Coordination and Rhythm	*Coordination* Gross body Hand dexterity Finger dexterity	*Coordination* Gross body Multiple limb		*Coordination* Gross motor Eye-hand Integration of both sides of body	*Coordination* Across body axis of different muscle groups simultaneously *Rhythm* Jerky vs. smooth movements Synchrony prerequisite (see Doll[5])
Speed and Agility	*Impulsion* General reaction time Tapping Articulation speed *Motor Speed* Arm-Hand-Finger	*Speed* Limb movement Running *Agility* Change of direction during movement	*Agility* Take-off Change of posture during movement	*Receipt and Propulsion* *Contact:* Reaching, grasping, releasing Manipulation to obtain information	*Speed* Continuous movement in space Running *Agility* Initiation of movement Change of direction
Flexibility	*Flexibility* Trunk Leg	*Flexibility – Speed*	*Flexibility* Spine and pelvis Shoulder girdle Bending forward and sideways	(Kephart uses the term flexibility for what is here defined as agility.)	*Flexibility* Maximum extension in trunk and limbs Rotation of joints

	Strength General Trunk Limbs	*Strength* Explosive Dynamic Static	*Strength* Shoulder girdle and arms Upper back Abdomen Legs		*Strength* General, specific muscle groups
Strength					
Endurance		*Endurance*			*Endurance* Sustained movement over time (see Cureton[6])
Balance	*Static Precision* Static balance Arm steadiness *Dynamic Precision* Dynamic balance Arm aiming Hand aiming	*Balance* Static Dynamic Object	*Balance* Movements on ground Movements on apparatus Movements while supported by another person	*Balance* Maintenance Dynamic relationship to gravity	*Balance* Static Dynamic Object

1. Guilford, J.P. A system of psychomotor abilities. *American Journal of Psychology*, 1958, **71**, 164-174.
2. Nicks, D.C., and Fleishman, E.A. What do physical tests measure — A review of factor analytic studies. Technical Report I, prepared for the Office of Naval Research by Yale University Departments of Industrial Administration and Psychology. New Haven: Yale Univ. Press, 1960.
3. Mosston, M. *Developmental Movement*. Columbus, Ohio: Charles E. Merrill, 1965.
4. Kephart, N.C. *The Slow Learner in the Classroom*. Columbus, Ohio: Charles E. Merrill, 1960. Also Godfrey B.B., and Kephart, N.C. *Movement Patterns and Motor Education*. New York: Appleton-Century-Crofts, 1969.
5. Doll, E. Neurophrenia. *American Journal of Psychiatry*, 1951, **108**, 50.
6. Cureton, T.K. 18-item motor fitness test. *Physical Fitness Workbook*. Champaign, Ill.: Univ. of Illinois Press, 1952.

Attributes Defined

A definition of each of the attributes of movement included in this program follows. Exercises for developing the attributes are given in Chapter 12.

Coordination

There is no agreement on the definition of coordination. Does it involve a single ability or several? Nicks and Fleishman (1960) suggest that the essence of coordination is the ability to integrate separate abilities into a complex task. In the present usage the term refers to the simultaneous and coordinated use of several muscles or muscle groups.

Both coordination and rhythm are characteristics of every movement, and this is probably why Mosston (1965) does not include them as a separate group in the specific movement skills that he specifies as the goals of training. We consider coordination as a separate entity, however, because some children show difficulty specifically with coordination, especially the coordination of both sides of the body. Exercises can be devised that train the ability to coordinate muscle groups while involving other movement skills to a lesser degree.

Nicks and Fleishman (1960) are of the opinion that good coordination depends upon the smooth functioning of the nervous system, with the cortex probably playing the major role. Ayres' studies support this view. She has published thorough studies (1965, 1966, 1967) on the role of the central nervous system in coordination. Neurologically handicapped children and children with learning difficulties frequently show poor motor coordination, especially in movements that involve crossing the midline of the body. They often cannot execute cross-lateral movements, such as moving the right leg and left arm simultaneously or walking sideways by crossing one leg behind the other. Kephart (1960) therefore regards cross-lateral exercises as most important (as his "Angels in the Snow" and other of his exercises attest).

Rhythm

The term rhythm as applied to movement denotes flowing, measured, balanced movement. It has two applications to movement education.

It may refer to the flow of movement with which a sequence is repeated — thus to a movement pattern. An example is smooth and graceful walking. If a person were to slip on a moist surface, stumble over the root of a tree, or collide with a water hydrant, the pattern would be broken. The walking would cease to be rhythmic.

Doll (1951) states that the ability to synchronize movements is the prerequisite for rhythmic movements. Rhythmic flow of movement depends upon good coordination. Exercises for training coordination therefore promote rhythmic movement also.

Rhythm may also refer to copying or creating reoccurring sequences of accented and nonaccented beats and units, either by sound with a percussion instrument, for example, or by body movement, such as clapping or stamping.

Flexibility

Flexibility involves the ability to move parts of the body easily in relation to each other, with a maximum range of joint extension and flexion. Flexibility is recognized in many physical education programs as an attribute of movement requiring specific training.*

An attempt is currently being made at the Frostig Center to measure the attributes of movement with a test battery developed by Sundstrom and Orpet (1968) and Orpet et al. (1968). According to the test results, flexibility is the only ability that diminishes rather than increases as a child grows older. It may be concluded that the physical education programs usually conducted in public schools do not provide sufficient training in flexibility. The increasing stiffness is exacerbated by many hours of sitting still in school and by lack of diversity in body movement. One may wonder if the lack of physical flexibility does not influence the personality also. One speaks of a person as being "flexible" or as being "rigid," "stiff," or "unbending."

Physical flexibility is achieved by movements requiring maximum extension of the joints, as, for instance, stunts and acrobatics. For example, somersaults increase the flexibility of the trunk forward.

Speed

Speed refers to the tempo achieved during a movement sequence. Speed does not refer to reaction time. Achieving a greater speed than other competitors is the main goal of various sports, such as competitive skiing, roller skating, track, and long distance running and swimming. In many other games and sports, from dodgeball

---

*Harris (1969) found no evidence that flexibility exists as a single general characteristic; his factor analytic study supported the hypothesis that flexibility is structured according to the body segment being used.

Five-year-olds learn to weave in and out between children on the floor without bumping them.

and Red Rover to football, handball, soccer, tennis, and polo, speed is a desirable attribute.

A child who is slow in his movements and cannot keep up with his age-mates will have difficulty in many of the sports and games enjoyed in school. Although speed is not as necessary in everyday life as it is in sports, the person who does not use reasonable speed is at a disadvantage. A slow moving child may be unable to finish his homework and may frequently arrive late in school; the slow housewife may take all day over her chores; and the slow worker may lose his job.

The causes of slowness in movement may be constitutional. Some people seem to be sluggish from infancy on; in others sluggishness can be linked to obesity; others may suffer from a disturbance in the functioning of the central nervous system because of brain damage, physical illness, or malnutrition. In any case in which physical causes are suspected, a medical referral is indicated for diagnosis and treatment.*

Slow moving children should be helped to become more aware of the flow of time. They should learn to compete with themselves in regard to the speed of assigned tasks. Exercises using locomotion,

*Some problems concerning the relationship of the movement education program to disturbances of the central nervous system are discussed in Chapter 9.

such as running in a circle, going over obstacle courses, skipping, hopping, and sidestepping, can be timed repeatedly. Other activities, such as setting up or putting away equipment, putting shoes on or taking them off, and copying directions for exercises, can also be timed to help make a slow moving child aware of his (hopefully) increasing speed in performing tasks. Eggtimers, clocks, and stopwatches can be used as timing instruments.

Emotional disturbances may also result in reduced speed. Children who are listless and lacking in zest tend to be slow; and the defeat experienced by slow children makes them more discouraged and further decreases their speed.

The teacher needs to take a slow moving child's feelings into account and use her relationship with the child to give him emotional support and encouragement.

Movement education lessons should always be so structured that they give such a child a feeling of success. The happier and more successful a slow moving child feels, the faster he tends to move. Observation of the child permits the teacher to discern those activities in which he is relatively successful, even if it is only a matter of being a fairly good ball monitor. The activities he enjoys and in which he is successful should be used with him frequently.

Agility

Agility is the capacity for fast reaction in body movement. It refers to the ability to initiate movement, change direction, or otherwise adjust position *speedily.*

Movement education exercises that promote agility are obstacle runs, work on gymnastic apparatus, those requiring a quick change of body position (such as quickly going from a sitting position on the floor to a standing position), rolling, and tumbling. Such exercises improve body control.

It has been observed that children who lack control of movement frequently lack control of general behavior, and conversely that controlled movement and controlled general behavior occur together. Research in the transfer of a behavior from one situation to others is always difficult, and there are no supporting statistics. It can be assumed, however, that better movement control will also help a child to control his general behavior more successfully.

Balance

Balance refers to the maintenance of a position with minimal contact with a surface. There are three kinds of balance — static, dynamic, and object.

Static balance refers to balance in which the support is stable and the person is not in locomotion. Standing on tiptoe is an example.

Dynamic balance involves the ability to maintain a position on a moving surface, as on a rolling ship, or while moving the body with minimal support, as on a balance board.

Object balance refers to supporting something minimally without letting it fall, as when a juggler balances a stick on his nose.

A most careful program for developing balance in children has been designed by Kephart (1960). In an article (1968) he gave an extensive list of variations in walking board exercises, which were developed by the State Health and Physical Education Department, Office of the Superintendent of Public Instruction, Springfield, Illinois.

Strength

Strength refers to force exerted either with the whole body or with parts of it. It is a term that can apply to specific muscle groups, as in gripping an object; or it can apply to the whole body, as in lifting a weight. Many exercises that to the layman do not seem to be particularly related to strength do, in fact, strengthen certain muscle groups. Jumping, for example, strengthens the leg muscles.

The lack of exercise or the restriction of exercise from which many children suffer results in weakness in the musculature. Adults, frequently by their own choice, share this disability. Many city dwellers shudder at the idea of taking a walk in the mountains or exploring on foot the lovely forests and seashores of our country. Their loss is not only physical but mental and spiritual.

Weak musculature of the legs and feet may result in pains that finally restrict freedom of locomotion to the point where walking becomes a chore. Weak musculature in other parts of the body may lead to other disabilities. For example, poor abdominal musculature can cause constipation and difficulties in childbirth and may contribute to scoliosis.

It is important for the teacher to be especially aware of the necessity for giving exercises to strengthen leg and foot muscles, back muscles, and abdominal muscles, as well as the muscles of the shoulder girdle and arms.

Endurance

There are two aspects of endurance: muscular and cardio-respiratory. Muscular endurance is the "ability to persist in physical activity and to resist muscular fatigue" (Devries, 1966). Cardio-respiratory endurance is the ability of the body to use oxygen in the most efficient way. Cureton (1965) and others discovered that not only the voluntary muscles but also the involuntary muscles, especially of the heart, can be exercised, and that heart disease and stroke may be prevented by physical exercise. They have thus helped make the present generation aware that endurance is significant for physical health in general — not only for sports and exploration.

Training in endurance requires extended sustained exercise. And since endurance training has to be fairly vigorous, it is not usually recommended for children under eight or nine years of age. Above this level, endurance exercises can be increasingly integrated into the program.

Extension of Movement

A further dimension of movement, which can be applied to each of the attributes of movement, is the degree of extension of a movement in space, or, to use another phrase, the degree of displacement of the body during movement. Four degrees of extension can be usefully differentiated.

Locomotion

Locomotion is the greatest degree of extension of movement, and it refers to change of locus of the body. Kephart (1960) refers to locomotion as a specific skill. Factor analysis has not identified locomotion as a movement skill. We therefore regard it as a form of movement.

Change in Body Position

Change in body position involves a change in the spatial relationships of the skeletal parts of the body to each other, as, for instance, moving from a sitting position to a standing position or from kneeling to lying.

Part Movements

Part movements refer to the use of parts of the body independently of other parts, as in manipulatory activities, such as lifting, holding, or turning objects; or nonmanipulatory activities, such as turning the head in order to see something.

Isometric Contractions

Isometric contractions are movements of the muscles only, without involving the skeletal structure of the body. Isometric exercises are designed to strengthen specific muscles. For instance, a strong, prolonged pull of the abdominal muscles strengthens those muscles and thus flattens the abdomen. Isometric exercises are discussed in Chapter 4.

A movement education program that takes into account both movement skills and degree of displacement in space will most likely include exercises for all muscle groups. If exercises requiring different body positions and extent of movement are included in the program, the teacher will have made a big step in developing a well balanced program.

Works Cited

Ayres, A. J. Interrelationships among perceptual-motor abilities in a group of normal children. *American Journal of Occupational Therapy,* 1966, **20**, 288-292.

Ayres, A. J. Interrelationships among perceptual-motor functions in children. *American Journal of Occupational Therapy,* 1966, **20**, 68-71.

Ayres, A. J. A neurobehavioral approach to evaluation and treatment of perceptual-motor dysfunction. Paper presented at the American Orthopsychiatric Association Annual Meeting, March 1967, Washington, D.C.

Ayres, A. J. Patterns of perceptual-motor dysfunction in children: A factor analytic study. *Perceptual and Motor Skills,* 1965, **20**, 335-368. (Monogr. Suppl. 1-V20.)

Barsch, R. H. *A Movigenic Curriculum.* Bulletin No. 25, Bureau for Handicapped Children. Madison, Wis.: State Department of Public Instruction, 1965.

Cureton, T. K. *Physical Fitness and Dynamic Health.* New York: Dial Press, 1965.

Devries, H. A. *Physiology of Exercise for Physical Education and Athletics.* Dubuque, Iowa: William C. Brown, 1966.

Doll, E. Neurophrenia. *American Journal of Psychiatry,* 1951, **108**, 50-53.

Getman, G. N. *How to Develop Your Child's Intelligence.* Luverne, Minn.: Author, 1962.

Godfrey, B. B., and Kephart, N. C. *Movement Patterns and Motor Education.* New York: Appleton-Century-Crofts, 1969.

Guilford, J. P. A system of psychomotor abilities. *American Journal of Psychology,* 1958, **71**, 164-174.

Harris, M. L. A factor analytic study of flexibility. *The Research Quarterly,* 1969, **40**, 62-70.

Kephart, N. C. *The Slow Learner in the Classroom.* Columbus, Ohio: Charles E. Merrill, 1960.

Kephart, N. C. Teaching the child with a perceptual-motor handicap. In M. Bortner (Ed.), *Evaluation and Education of Children with Brain Damage.* Springfield, Ill.: C. C. Thomas, 1968.

Laban, R. *Modern Educational Dance.* (2nd rev. ed.) New York: Praeger, 1968. (First published 1948.)

Los Angeles City School Districts. *Physical Education Teaching Guide.* Division of Instructional Services, Publication No. 472. Los Angeles: 1957.

Mosston, M. *Developmental Movement.* Columbus, Ohio: Charles E. Merrill, 1965.

Mosston, M. *Teaching Physical Education.* Columbus, Ohio: Charles E. Merrill, 1966.

Nicks, D. C., and Fleishman, E. A. What do physical tests measure – A review of factor analytic studies. Technical Report I, prepared for the Office of Naval Research by Yale University Departments of Industrial Administration and Psychology. New Haven: Yale Univ. Press, 1960.

Orpet, R., Sundstrom, P., and Pollach, S. A factor analysis of sensory-motor abilities of elementary school children. Paper presented at the meeting of the California Educational Research Association, March 1968, Oakland.

Sonoma County Schools. A segmented demonstration physical education program, No. 2645, Title III, P. L. 89-10. Santa Rosa, Calif.: Office of the Superintendent, 1969.

Sundstrom, P., and Orpet, R. Factor analysis of sensory-motor abilities in children with learning disabilities. Paper presented at the meeting of the California Association of School Psychologists and Psychometrists, March 1968, Oakland.

Chapter 4

Body Awareness

Body awareness is essential for normal psychological and physical development. Without it a child cannot realize that he is an independent being, separate from the world around him; that he is an "I," or, as he expresses it at an early age, a "me."

Definition and Analysis of Body Awareness

The relationship of body awareness to the total physical and emotional adjustment of the human being has been widely studied; and neurologists, psychiatrists, psychologists, and educators agree on its importance. But scholars part company concerning the definition of body awareness. The term body awareness appears frequently in educational literature, but it is used by different authors for a variety of phenomena and is rarely defined. Ajuriaguerra (1965) differentiates between the cognitive aspect of the body (that is, the perception and knowledge of the body) and its affective aspect, "the body as it is felt." Witkin (1949) does not make this differentiation. He uses the term body image and endows it with both meanings. Schilder (1964) uses body image and body schema interchangeably. Head (1920) uses the phrase "postural model of the body," which would seem to be congruent with the term body schema as used in this book, but he includes many of the characteristics differentiated under body image in this book. The variations in the use of these terms make it necessary to define them for our purposes.

The various symptoms associated with disturbances in body awareness suggest that different functions may be involved. For the purpose of this movement education program, three functions are differentiated: body image, body schema, and body concept. This tripartite division, although to a certain degree artificial, is based on clinical observation, and its purpose is to provide a useful model for constructing developmental and remedial educational programs.

Body Image

Body image is defined as the sum of all feelings concerning the body, "the body as it is felt," to use Ajuriaguerra's phrase. It has its roots in very early experiences — the feeling of being warm or cold, satiated or hungry, comfortable or uncomfortable, in sucking, touching, and being touched. The body image is further shaped and influenced by the totality of the life experiences and thought processes through which the world is recognized and through which the individual recognizes himself; and by all the feelings and emotions through which the human being relates to the world around him. Body image is strongly influenced by the physical characteristics of a person, his feelings about himself, his perception of how others feel about him, and by his moods and attitudes. All afferent stimuli — that is, all stimuli directed toward the central nervous system — contribute to body image, but of special importance are those that come from inside the body and from the surface of the body.

Ayres (1965) states that a disturbance in body image may be due to a failure to register kinesthetic stimuli (stimuli that originate from the functions of the muscles) or tactile stimuli that originate from the skin. This assumption is well documented by research and points to the importance of haptic (kinesthetic and tactile) stimulation. But the body image is influenced by all aspects of a child's development — sensory-motor functions, communicative abilities, perception, intellectual grasp, emotional development, and social adjustment.

Clinical observations indicate that deficits in body image and in visual perception frequently occur together. Ayres (1965) is probably correct when she concludes that lack of body awareness — not lack of movement skills — leads to disturbances of visual perception.* The visual perceptual deficiences further affect the body image.

Disturbances in body image are manifested by faulty figure drawing. When a child consistently makes self-portraits without parts of the body, draws himself very small because he feels so little and insignificant, or draws himself immensely huge because he wishes he could gain control of a threatening universe, he is also reflecting the emotional disturbance that may either accompany or cause disturbed body image.

A child's verbal expressions may also testify to this distortion of body image as the authors' experiences with varying pathologies attest. One five-year-old asserted that she could fit into the water

---

*Ayres (1967) states, "Disorders are interpreted in terms of dysfunction of sensory integrative mechanisms at several levels of the brain." In other words, her research and clinical findings support the contention that input (perception) and the integration of input is more crucial than output (motor performance) for general adaptation and learning. Hunt (1961) is of the same opinion.

pipe under the sink and take refuge inside; another that his brain had a rotten part; another that his head was cracked (literally); another that his head could be screwed off, shrunken, and replaced; another that he was so strong that if he really tried to shake his house it would fall down; and still another that his brain sent out powerful rays. Other more common examples often found among so-called normal children are those in which the children, although of average or better than average appearance, believe themselves to be ugly or queerly shaped.

The close relationship between body image and self image is discussed by Johnson (1962): "(1) . . . both are important with respect to the effectiveness of the personality throughout life; (2) body-image and self-concept may mean the same thing in early life when the child is his body and additional personality resources on which to build a self-concept are not yet available; and (3) it should be possible to improve the body-image and thus especially in childhood and perhaps in old age to improve the entire self-concept — by enhancing neuromuscular control and physiological fitness."

Corrective emotional experiences, as well as movement education, may therefore be needed to influence the body image. Although the teacher is rarely a trained psychotherapist, she can provide a therapeutic environment. She can amend a child's feelings about himself by encouraging a supportive classroom atmosphere, by fostering good relationships with other children and with herself, and by providing opportunities for expression. Above all, it is important that children experience success.

Since a child's body image reflects his total development, all experiences with the curriculum affect it. Movement education provides the most direct means of enhancing body image.

This child is "round like a ball." She learns to change her shape during creative movement.

Body Schema

The term body schema as used here refers to automatic adjustment of the skeletal parts and to the tensing and relaxing of muscles necessary to maintain a position, to move without falling, and to move other objects efficiently.

A child is born with reflexes that relate his posture to the environment — for example, the tonic neck reflex and the grasping reflex. The body schema develops further as a child learns to maintain a position at will and to move, crawl, stand up, walk, and adjust his skeletal parts automatically and continuously so that he does not lose balance or fall while engaging in change of body position or in locomotion.

It is rather difficult to differentiate between body image and body schema in the healthy person. But a split between body image and schema can be observed in pathological states, and the differentiation has important implications for education. To illustrate the difference, in temporary sensory deprivation, the body image is disturbed but not the body schema. A person has no difficulty in moving after a period of sensory deprivation, but disturbances in his feelings about his body may persist for some time. A psychotic person may have strange ideas or feelings concerning his body without being visibly handicapped in his movements. Minimally brain damaged children also often have distorted body images, as shown by their figure drawings, which commonly have abnormally large heads and often show other misconceptions. This faulty self-perception is not always paralleled by movement or posture difficulties.* Intoxication by drugs such as LSD also distorts the body image without measurably effecting changes in body schema. The difference between body image and body schema as defined here can therefore be observed in sensory deprivation, in psychosis, in certain cases of brain damage, and in some states of intoxication.

Disturbances of body schema are much more pronounced than those of body image in many cases of general neurological impairment (cerebral palsy, for instance) and in local disturbances of the vestibular function. They are manifested in a child's faulty movement patterns, especially in movements in which the midline of the body is crossed and in movements requiring a high degree of coordination.

---

*Examples are the distortions of body image reported on pages 44-45.

Another symptom is the inability to move certain parts of the body at will. For instance, George, a nine-year-old boy of average intelligence with no restriction in his ability to move, could not bend his knee when asked to do so. He had to be actively shown by the instructor before he could learn to bend the knee by himself as directed.

Disturbances in body schema also include disturbances of laterality and directionality. Many children with learning difficulties cannot differentiate between right and left directions, even at intermediate and secondary grade levels. Body image disturbances are also involved in the difficulty of differentiating between the right and left sides of the body when the definition "the body as it is felt" is used for body image. As has already been mentioned, disturbances of coordination of movements of the right and left sides of the body are frequent. Children with this disturbance, for instance, may not be able to move at will the right hand and the left leg at the same time.

Disturbances in body schema are treated by movement education or physiotherapy, especially through procedures that make a child aware of the changes, adaptations, and regulation of his posture. For specific exercises, see this chapter, pages 55-56. If a child is conscious of his posture and movements, he can adjust them more readily to various tasks. The coach who shows a person how to dribble a ball, hold a racquet, or swing a golf club addresses himself to the body schema (in the present definition) and not to the body image.

Body Concept

Fortunately the differentiation of body concept from body image and body schema can be demonstrated without recourse to pathological states. Body concept refers to the factual knowledge of the body — to the knowledge that a human being has two eyes, two shoulders joining the arms to the body, two legs, and so on.

The child who draws the human figure with four legs indicates that his body concept is faulty, as well as his body image. The same may be true of the child who cannot locate a body part on himself, on others, or in a picture. But a child may have excellent body image and body schema and still know little about his anatomy or body functions.

A child's body concept is developed by giving him information about his body. During the elementary school years, children should acquire the basic facts of human physiology. They should learn about the digestive, circulatory, nervous, and other systems. This subject matter can easily be conveyed in the course of a movement education program, but the teacher should not encroach on the time needed for physical exercise.

Research in Body Awareness

Since the inception of the concept of body image and the initial observations of changes in body perception in pathology (Head, 1920; Schilder, 1964), research has continued, but little has permeated the educational literature or has been systematically applied to education.

Witkin et al. (1962) and Wapner and Werner (1957) summarized studies of the perception of the body and the environment by both children and adults resulting from changes in environmental variables (for example, tilt of the room), or changes in body position in a stable environment, or changes in body position and environment. For example, subjects were seated in complete darkness, facing a luminous rod surrounded by a luminous frame. Rod and frame could be independently tilted. While the frame remained tilted, the subject was required to move the rod until it appeared vertical. The subject was asked to do this while the position of his head and the position of his body were varied systematically (Witkin and Asch, 1948). To evaluate the individual's perception of the position of his body and of the whole surrounding field, Witkin and his colleagues used a special room with a special chair. The chair and the entire room could be tilted together or separately (apparatus first described by Witkin, 1949). The subject was asked to move the chair within the tilted room to a position where he felt himself seated upright. Witkin (1950) also studied the effect of changing the direction of force on the body by means of a rotating room apparatus.

This extensive series of studies showed that there were marked individual differences in the way people orient themselves in space toward the upright. Some subjects seemed to rely primarily on visual cues — on the appearance of the field in relation to the body. Others seemed to base their judgments primarily on body sensations. Witkin calls the former, who find it difficult to overcome the influence of the surrounding field, field dependent. The latter he calls field independent. He hypothesized that the two types resulted from differences in ability to overcome the distraction resulting from the context in which an object is perceived. This hypothesis has been supported by many succeeding studies (see Witkin et al., 1962, pp. 43ff.), including tests in which the individual is asked to find embedded figures in a drawing. Witkin states that the common element in these test situations is that the subject is required to separate an item (his body, a rod, or a design) from its background or context. In other words, figure-ground perception is involved in all of them.

Witkin et al. (1954), as well as Wapner and Werner (1957), found that children become more field independent as they grow older,* but that some children consistently behave like younger children and are more field dependent than their age-mates. Witkin et al. (1962) found, moreover, that field dependency interferes with intellectual performance because the field dependent person cannot isolate essential elements from material presented and combine them into new relationships. Field dependent children lack analytic ability, and their IQ scores tend therefore to be lower. He describes the field independent child as being superior in the following respects: He has a better concept of his body, a better sense of his own identity, more awareness of the outside world and of his own needs, better control and self-direction, and he can channel his impulses more effectively. He is purposeful, active, and goal directed. He tends to have better scores in the block design, object assembly, and picture completion subtests on the Wechsler Intelligence Scale for Children.

Witkin and his colleagues believe field dependency or independency is a trait that can be modified by the environment. They believe that family experiences influence the environment and therefore influence the perception of the body and the outer world. (They do not discuss other environmental influences.) But the important question for the teacher is whether education and school experiences can influence body awareness.

Few controlled research studies, if any, have been carried out to show that a modification of body awareness can be achieved by educational means; or that if such changes were wrought, they would subsequently modify a child's total behavior. Nevertheless, Kephart (1968), Barsch (1965), Cohen and Berger (1966), and others are convinced that the curriculum for children with learning difficulties should be based on a sensory-motor program that promotes the development of visual perception and kinesthetic awareness. The descriptions of neurologically handicapped children with whom these educators work indicate that the children fit the description of extremely field dependent children and that they lack body awareness. They overreact to external stimuli, neglecting kinesthetic stimuli.

---

*Ajuriaguerra (1965) points out that the changes that occur in children as they grow older may be what Piaget (1966) has described as decentration, a change in perceptual behavior not necessarily connected with body awareness. Although Ajuriaguerra may be correct, the interdependence of body awareness and awareness of the environment has been proved (Ayres, 1965).

Our clinical observations clearly indicate that some of the characteristics that endanger a child's adaptation to the environment are highly correlated with, and most probably influenced by, inadequate body awareness. Perception of the environment and awareness of the body are interdependent. Perceptual training and movement education are therefore of equal importance. The basic approach of such educators as Kephart and Barsch, who try to modify a child's development by emphasizing both sensory-motor and perceptual tasks, is therefore a sound one. But it is important to be aware that although both kinds of tasks are related, they are separate and require equally comprehensive training.

The conclusions that seem inescapable from all of the research studies and observations are that disturbances in body image occur frequently in children; that body image may influence a child's emotional well-being, his learning ability, and his intellectual performance; and that body image can be modified by training.*

Developing Body Image

All conscious body movement develops some aspect of body awareness. Free movement and creative expression (Chapter 5) are effective in promoting body awareness because in creative movement the body becomes the expressive instrument, like clay for the sculptor or the violin for the musician. For many children, free creative movement is sufficient to enhance the awareness of the body "as it is felt." But the point of view of the authors is that many other children need very specific exercises such as those described in this chapter.

The exercises that follow are not "therapeutic," that is, not designed only for children with disturbances of body image. They may be used with all children in both regular and special classes unless there are specific medical contraindications.

Isometric Exercises

Isometric exercises use muscular tension to strengthen specific muscle groups. The muscle groups are maximally tensed, the tension is held for a few seconds, and the muscles are then relaxed. Relaxation

---

*See, for example, Johnson, W. R., Fretz, B. R., and Johnson, J. A. Changes in self-concepts during a physical development program. *The Research Quarterly,* 1968, 39, 560-565; Painter, G. The effects of a rhythmic and sensory-motor activity program on perceptual motor spatial abilities of kindergarten children. *Exceptional Children,* 1966, 33, 113-116.

should immediately follow every exercise in which tension is used. Exercises for relaxation follow the isometric exercises.

Exercises marked with an asterisk should be performed with eyes closed and eyes open. With eyes closed, a child is able to concentrate on kinesthetic (muscular) feedback without interference from visual stimuli.

1. The children interlace fingers of both hands. Press palms hard together. Hold while the teacher counts to three; relax pressure. Repeat.

2. The children bend head to one side, keeping face forward so that maximum tension is felt in the neck muscles of the opposite side. Keep other body parts still. Hold while the teacher counts to three; relax; return to original position. Bend to the other side.

3. The children bend head forward so that maximum tension is felt in the back neck muscles. Keep other body parts still. Hold while the teacher counts to three; relax; return to original position. Bend head backward. (Do not use Exercises 3 and 4 on the same day.)

4. The children sit on the floor cross-legged, hands behind neck, fingers interlaced. Press with hands against neck and, rounding the back, bend forward as far as possible, pressing neck down with the hands. Hold while the teacher counts to three. Repeat; lie on floor; relax. (Do not use Exercises 3 and 4 on the same day.)

5. The children lie on the back on the floor. Knees may be bent slightly. Stretch arms and hands forward; raise head, neck, and shoulders from the floor. Hold while the teacher counts to three. Relax.

6. The children lie on the back on the floor, knees bent, feet flat. Contract abdomen. Hold and breathe in and out deeply three times. Relax.

7. The children sit on the floor, hips and knees bent, feet on floor (hook position). Shift weight backward onto lower back, letting feet rise from floor. At the same time bend head and shoulders forward. Hold while the teacher counts to three. Return to sitting position without using hands.

*8. Raising the head and chest while lying on the floor must be avoided with children who tend to have swaybacks. A better exercise for such children is one in which they contract the back muscles without bending the spine back. For example, a child lies facedown on a table or bench so that his hips are supported. The teacher holds his ankles. His upper trunk bends forward over the edge of the table, with legs supported horizontally. The child raises head and back so that his entire body is parallel to floor. Hold as long as possible (up to the count of three).

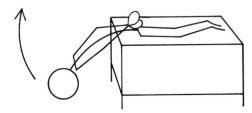

Relaxation Exercises

*1. The children try to "melt" into the floor while both supine and prone.

*2. The children sit on the floor, and each pretends he is a rag doll and sinks to the floor, or he pretends he is sand that runs out of a bag.

3. The children practice falling like rag dolls from standing position. At first this should only be done on a mat and after the children have been shown how a rag doll falls. (The teacher demonstrates with a rag doll.)

*4. While "melting" into the floor or during any rest period, children can become aware of the rhythmic activity of inner organs by concentrating on the sensations produced by heartbeat and breathing.

Additional relaxation and breathing exercises are in Chapter 12.

Tactile Stimulation Exercises Using Resistance

*1. The children press against the floor or other rigid surface with the whole body in both supine and prone positions.

2. The children kneel with hands on floor below shoulders and slightly turned inward, thighs at right angles to the floor, back straight. They try to press "holes" in the floor with hands. Hold while the teacher counts to three. Relax.

3. The children stand with back about four to six inches from wall. Lean backward and press against the wall with back as hard as possible. Still pressing, slide down to a position as if sitting on a chair, with knees bent and back flat against the wall. Slide up to original position.

4. The children stand about ten inches from the wall, facing it. They lean toward it and pretend to push it back with their hands.

Tactile Stimulation Exercises with Resilient Resistance

1. Two children stand back to back. One child pushes forward; the other provides resistance but only to the degree that he is pushed slowly across the room. Reverse the roles.

2. Two children stand facing each other, palms touching. One child pushes the other backward; the other provides resistance, as in Exercise 1. Reverse the roles.

3. The children are paired. One child is a horse; the other a wagon. One child stands behind the other but both face the same direction. They clasp hands, and the child in front, the horse, pulls the other across the room. The child who is the wagon makes himself "heavy."

Tactile Stimulation Exercise with Body Passive

This exercise is done by children in pairs during a rest period. One child lies on the floor; the other kneels near him holding a stick with a ball of cotton on the end. The teacher calls out the names of body parts. For example: toe . . . knee . . . hair . . . knee . . . nose . . . hip . . . stomach . . . shinbone . . . cheek . . . thigh . . . neck . . . knee . . . chest . . . cheek . . . toe . . . knee . . . foot . . . arm . . . ear . . . fingers . . . forehead . . . ankle. The kneeling child lightly touches the body parts of the other child with the cotton ball as the teacher calls them out.

Some children may not like to be touched by the cotton ball and may show fear or aversion. Reassure such children that they are not required to do the exercise if they do not feel comfortable with it.

Apparatus Exercises

The Trampoline. In *The Slow Learner in the Classroom,* Kephart points out that trampoline exercises develop body image. A child becomes aware of his body because of the difference in gravitational pull while he is in the air. He is thrown upward by the trampoline, and the upward pull then changes into a downward pull. This necessitates a continuous adjustment of muscle tensions during the jump. Kephart also correctly observes another advantage of the trampoline — the enjoyment it provides. Trampolines are not always available. In their absence, Kephart suggests using bedsprings to which a mattress is securely tied.

At the Center we have found trampoline boards (see Chapter 10, page 157, for a description) particularly helpful. They are relatively inexpensive, portable, and far safer than the regular trampoline. They provide most of the same benefits: coordination of large muscle groups, balance, and sensitivity to the movements of others when the children work in pairs. We have found that the most severely motor-handicapped youngster enjoys the trampoline board as much as other children, and that its use becomes an excellent motivating factor. Many children who have never been "airborne" because they cannot jump are delighted with the trampoline board.

Cratty (1969) points out several other ways in which exercises on the trampoline help to develop body image. A child may become more aware of the position of his body relative to up-down, right-left, and back-front when he experiences the feeling of weightlessness as he bounces into the air from the trampoline. He may become better able to locate specific body parts, especially those involved in first contact with the surface on the return. He may also better understand the difference between size and length of various body segments as differences in the distances of falls are experienced.

Other Apparatus.   The climbing, swinging, and sliding that are made possible by other playground apparatus share some of the characteristics of the trampoline exercises in that gravitational pull is modified in a rhythmic way. Another factor in improving the body image is the tactile stimulation that the use of the apparatus provides.

The gravitational pull is also modified in movements that do not require the use of apparatus, such as jumping, skipping, leaping, galloping, turning, tumbling, and especially whirling and dancing, where centrifugal force comes into play. Apparatus is therefore not essential, but it contributes to acquisition of skills and to children's enjoyment (see Chapter 10).

Exercises Combining Tactile and Kinesthetic Stimulation

1. The children crawl through a tunnel.
2. The children roll on the floor.
3. The children do somersaults. The teacher must ensure that the children do this properly so as to avoid any possible injury to the neck muscles. An inexperienced or young child often attempts to straighten his neck just before rolling so that the body weight is borne on the neck instead of the shoulders. The teacher should at first assist the child by placing one hand on the child's buttocks and the other on the nape of the neck, lifting the child over and down while at the same time keeping the child's head tucked under.
4. The children use light weights. If the children wear armbands or ankle bands with small lead weights sewn into them or carry objects in their hands or on head or back, the usual forces acting on

the body are changed and the children's awareness of the weighted body part is increased.

Exercises in Avoiding Collisions

In the foregoing exercises, body awareness was promoted through touch. The following exercises promote body image through the children's becoming aware of body boundaries in relation to objects that they must avoid.

1. An obstacle course (see page 158) can bring the body in various relationships with high and low, wide and narrow, round and angular, and big and small objects. Obstacle courses can also be used in the exercises using creative movement, discussed in Chapter 5.

Obstacle courses may be formed in the classroom as well as on the playground. (With small children they may be called an over-under game.) The children can be told to crawl under a table, step over a chair, jump over lines drawn on the floor, go around other children, and so on. When the children are familiar with an obstacle course, the teacher may time their performances in order to promote agility and speed, in addition to body image.

2. The children run different directions in a circumscribed area, avoiding collisions.

3. The children play dodgeball.

As previously emphasized, body image is closely related to a child's perception of himself as a person. The teacher therefore needs to promote an emotional climate in the classroom that makes each child feel secure and adequate. This is so important in the development of body image that another reminder is necessary: Kindliness, friendliness, and consideration should be the hallmarks of the classroom. Children should be encouraged to give each other support and emotional warmth. The child who is a loner needs extra support and attention, encouragement, praise, and recognition from the teacher. The child who is shy should be encouraged to integrate with the group, but he should not be forced. Some children need to work by themselves at first and then in pairs before they can join in a group exercise.

Developing Body Schema

To repeat our definition, body schema refers to the automatic adjustment of the skeletal parts of the body and to the tensing and relaxing of muscles necessary to maintain a position, to move without falling, and to move other objects efficiently. All exercises for the development of body image involve body schema also. In fact, all movements help to develop body schema to a certain degree.

Specific exercises for body schema are those that require precise or rapid skeletal adjustment and those in which a child becomes aware of his body position, as when copying a body position.

The game of This Is It serves this purpose. The children first practice assuming different positions — such as being small, tall, or middle-size, or having one, two, three, four, five, or six points on the ground, or having their bodies turned toward the ground or the sky, forward, backward, twisted, and so on. They watch each other's positions. When they have learned a large repertoire of different positions, the children take turns in being leader. The leader assumes a position and shouts "This is it!" and the other children have to adopt the same position. This game, incidentally, also provides training in visual-motor association (see Chapter 7).

Postural and balance exercises, such as those suggested by Kephart (1960), and exercises requiring agility are also of special value in promoting body schema.

Finally, exercises that help children with awareness of right and left and with the integration of both sides of the body also develop body schema. These exercises are discussed in the following section.

Laterality and Directionality

According to Harris (1958), lateral dominance refers to the preference for or superiority of one side of the body over the other in performing motor tasks. A right-dominant person, therefore, is one who prefers to use the right hand, right eye, and right foot. The left-dominant person prefers to use the left hand, left eye, and left foot.

Some children, however, prefer to use the left hand but the right eye and the right foot, or the right hand and the right eye but the left foot, for example. This is referred to as crossed dominance. Another variation in lateral dominance occurs when a child uses the right or left hand alternatingly, a condition referred to as unestablished dominance, or mixed dominance (Harris, 1958).

The relationship between laterality and learning ability, especially in reading, is still a very controversial issue, but it seems likely that the controversy stems in part from a confusion in terminology. Laterality is sometimes thought to mean the same as lateral dominance and sometimes the same as directionality. This is an error. *Directionality* refers to the knowledge of left and right in space; *laterality,* to knowledge of the left and right sides of the body; *lateral dominance* to the preferred side of the body. Hunter (1968) refers to laterality as

These children thoroughly enjoy dancing and jumping in pairs. They learn to work together and enhance their coordination and rhythm.

the "map of inner space," and to directionality as the "map of outer space."

Directionality and laterality do have an effect upon learning ability, but not lateral dominance. Children who have no knowledge of the right and left directions in their books or on their papers have difficulties in learning. Orientation on a page is necessary in reading consistently from left to right, in writing letters in the correct direction, and in writing numbers. In contrast, our research and that of others indicates that modification of lateral dominance is not always related to learning. For example, crossed dominance is *not* correlated with reading ability.

Belmont and Birch (1965) and Trieschmann (1968) found no differences in lateral dominance characteristics between children with reading difficulties and their controls. Balow (1963) found that hand dominance and reading achievement were unrelated in first graders. Cohen and Glass (1968), Nichols (1959), and Rabinovitch, Drew, DeJong, Ingram, and Withey (1956) have all found right-left confusion but not lateral preference to affect reading. Johnson and Myklebust (1967) wrote that in studies by Benton (1959) and Ilg and Ames (1965) it was found that the ability to judge right from left is frequently disturbed in children with psychoneurological learning disabilities, but they did not report finding differences in laterality (dominance) characteristics.

On the other hand, Orton (1961), Harris (1957), Zangwill (1962), and Silver and Hagin (1967) have suggested that ambiguity regarding laterality is a direct cause of congenital dyslexia. It should be affirmed that these authors do not include crossed dominance as a cause of learning difficulties.

No inference regarding cerebral dominance can be made from observation of laterality of hand, eye, or foot (Zangwill, 1962). Goodglass and Quadfasel (1954) have shown that cerebral dominance for language is not entirely correlated with dominance for motor skills. Moreover, change in hand dominance does not affect brain dominance.

In summary, the role of lateral dominance is disputed, and evidence seems to make a direct causal connection between lateral dominance and learning difficulties questionable.

Our view is probably most clearly stated by Reinhold (1963): "Perhaps our whole notion of dominance, so closely allied to representation of functions, is fallacious. In order to read or write, it is necessary to distinguish right from left. Orientation and direction, progressive movement and memory are all necessary in reading and writing.*"

We, however, believe that unestablished (mixed) dominance may have an indirect effect upon learning because the lack of preference for one hand inhibits the knowledge of right and left and can cause confused directionality, which many studies show to be related to learning ability. If dominance is established, the consistent use of one hand strengthens the muscles in the hand and arm and probably causes a different tonus pull in the arm. This distinctive kinesthetic feeling characterizes the dominant hand, and it therefore leads to immediate knowledge of which side is left and which is right. Children lacking this kinesthetic guide are handicapped in acquiring directionality. It is therefore important to use movement education both for teaching directionality directly and for establishing hand dominance.

As Cratty (1969) states, proper training can lead to transfer between dominance and directionality and in turn to enhanced learning of academic skills: "With innumerable left-right movement experiences and the proper building of a cognitive bridge between this kind of left-right concept and the left and right of space we may aid children to reverse letters less, and in other ways to correctly order letters in words and words in phrases. You must say to Johnny 'See the "d" faces toward your left hand' rather than leaving to chance the transfer of left-right movement activities and the correct ordering of the left and right of space.†"

The teacher should also understand that left-handedness is not properly regarded as causing learning difficulties, and that crossed

---

*Used by permission of the Royal Society of Medicine.
†Used by special permission of John Wiley & Sons, Inc.

dominance is probably the rule rather than the exception in young children. It is important for the teacher of movement education to realize that establishing eye-hand dominance is a maturational phenomenon,* and that children with perceptual-motor maturity will tend to show established dominance (Flick, 1966).

Many studies, for example, Rudel and Teuber (1963), indicate that both immature motor patterns and directionality can be influenced by training. Movement education can help to ameliorate the general immaturity of motor functions and help develop the perception of right and left.

Exercises for Laterality (Dominance)

The following procedures are helpful for strengthening the muscle tonus in the dominant hand, thus establishing laterality.

1. Kephart† recommends that children with poor tonus pull in both arms wear a weighted armband on the arm that is expected to be dominant.†† The armband is a strip of cloth into which are sewn six to eight fish weights of about one ounce each. It is worn for about 30 minutes a day, during writing as well as during movement education.

2. A child makes a fist by clenching the dominant hand as strongly as possible and then bends the elbow and tries to flex the muscles in the upper arm. He holds the position for three seconds and then stretches the arm. Repeat two or three times.

3. A child lifts a heavy sandbag, using the dominant arm *only*.

Exercises for Directionality (Right-left discrimination)

A child with difficulties in directionality should at first be provided with some fixed cue to help him establish which his right hand is and which his left is. This may be done with a weighted armband (as recommended by Kephart), with one without weights, or by making a mark such as a dot or sign or small picture drawn on the appropriate hand with a crayon or decal. Every paper that the child receives in the classroom should have a small mark in the upper left-hand corner so that he readily identifies the left side of the paper and knows from which side to begin writing. If a small arrow pointing to the right is drawn at the upper left-hand corner of the paper, it will help the child to initiate the correct movement.

---

*Isom (1969) has found, in a longitudinal study of several hundred children, that between the ages of four and seven 20 percent change "eyedness" and 10 percent change "handedness."

†   Oral communication

†† If careful testing and observation reveal no hand preference, a child should be taught to use the right hand.

During movement education, the following exercises, given in order of difficulty, are helpful. Only one exercise should be used in a session.

1. The children are separated into two groups — right- and left-handed children. Every right-handed child is given a beanbag to hold in his right hand; every left-handed child is given a beanbag to hold in his left hand. (This promotes a different muscle tonus in the dominant hand.) The exercise is carried out with the right-handed group as follows: When the teacher says "Right!" each child raises his right arm slowly forward to the horizontal position and slowly says "Right." The arm is then lowered. Repeat five times. The teacher should take care not to intrude other words such as *up* or *down.* When the children can do this satisfactorily, the teacher may use a drum or tambourine to give the signal for the children to raise their arms and say "Right."

The same exercise is done by the left-handed children, who respond with left arms to the word "Left!"

2. The right- and left-handed groups are again separated, but the exercise is done without beanbags. The teacher says slowly to the right-handed group: "Right arm, point right." Each child slowly raises his right arm forward until it is parallel with the floor; then he slowly swings it around until he is pointing to the side, the index finger outstretched. Again the children accompany the action with words: "Point right." Subsequently the teacher can give a signal instead of saying the words. Repeat five times.

The left-handed children learn to point left.

3. The teacher explains and demonstrates what a quarter-turn is and what a half-turn is. This exercise is similar to Exercise 2, but a third step is added. The teacher says slowly to the right-handed group, "Turn right," and the children make a quarter-turn to the right, but they do not move the arm that is pointing to the right. Thus they finish the movement facing in the same direction as the arm is pointing. The children say "Turn right" as they do it.

The left-handed group turns left.

The following exercises are for more advanced children.

4. The teacher explains that by jumping a half-turn a child faces the opposite side of the room or circle. If a child needs to take two jumps to face the opposite side, each jump is only a quarter-turn. The children should practice making quarter- and half-turn jumps according to the teacher's directions.

After practice, a game may be played in which one child gives the directions for jumping. For example: "Half-turn right, quarter-turn left, quarter-turn right." If a child fails to carry out the directions correctly, he becomes "It," and he gives the directions until another child fails.

5. This is similar to Exercise 3, but the children make the quarter-turn four times — until they return to the initial position, facing the teacher. After a few days of practice, the right-handed group should be taught to raise the left arm and turn left, the left-handed group to raise the right arm and turn right. When each group is able to turn in either direction according to the signal, the two groups can do the exercise together. Each group turns in the direction of the dominant hand when the signal "Turn" is given.

6. Jack Be Nimble, Jack Be Quick: Blocks, rods, or beanbags representing candlesticks are placed on the floor or ground to form a course. Each child, in turn, proceeds from the starting place to the goal by jumping over the "candlesticks." After jumping the first, a child should turn toward the second, saying in which direction he has turned. He continues over the course, each time saying in which direction he has turned. The course should be so arranged that the children must make both left and right turns.

7. This is a more elaborate version of Exercise 6. Because it involves surmounting obstacles, it promotes body image and perception of spatial relationships, as well as directionality.

Each child, in turn, follows a chalkline until he encounters an obstacle that is set either to the right or to the left of the line. He stretches his arm to the side in the direction of the obstacle and turns toward it, saying the direction in which he is turning. For example, he might say "The rock is to my right. I turn to the right. I climb over the rock." The obstacle could be a small rock, a rope tied between two chairs (which may be climbed over or crawled under), a stick held between two children, a suspended tire (to be crawled through), a balance beam (to go over or walk on), a block, or a chair.

8. This game involves identifying the left and right sides of the body, crossing the midline, and identifying the various body parts.

The children sit on the floor, knees bent, feet flat on the floor. The teacher calls out directions for the children to follow, such as: "Right hand on left knee; cross arms in front of chest; left hand on right knee; cross arms in front of chest; right hand on left eye; cross arms; left hand on right hip; cross arms; right hand on left hip; cross arms; right hand on left ear; cross arms; left hand on right ear; cross arms; right hand on left foot; cross arms; left hand on right foot; cross arms."

The children repeat each direction after the teacher. If crossing arms is too difficult, the children may put their arms at their sides.

When the children become proficient, they can be asked to perform the exercise rapidly, but they need not say the directions aloud. This exercise may help to reduce the reaction time for slow moving children and train them in receptive and expressive language. Another group of exercises important for development of awareness of right and left are mirror images, exercises that should be used only with children who are older than six.*

Directionality needs to be practiced throughout the school day. Left-to-right movement is necessary in reading and writing. Conscious emphasis on directions may be included in arithmetic, art, general classroom directions, and so on.

Developing Body Concept

By body concept is meant the factual knowledge a person has of his body (see page 47). As body concept includes all conscious knowledge about the body, the teacher should discuss the functions and the anatomy of the organs and of the body systems, and she should give some time to questions of health.

Exercise for Body Concept

The following exercise, similar to Exercise 8 for directionality, is designed to give practice in recognizing and locating body parts.

The children stand. The teacher says: "Clap twice; put your elbows together; put your feet apart; touch one elbow; touch both elbows; put your knees together; touch your right knee with your left hand; touch your left knee with your right hand; touch your nose; touch your toes with your arms crossed; touch your nose with one hand, your knee with the other; put your hands on your head; touch one knee and one foot; clap once; place your palms together; touch one shoulder; clasp your hands behind your neck; clap once; draw a square in the air; touch your eyes; touch your heels; put your left hand on your left toe; put your left hand on your right toe."

---

*Discussed in *Teacher's Guide for Intermediate Pictures and Patterns* (Frostig and Horne, 1966).

Works Cited

Ajuriaguerra, J. Discussion. In S. Wapner and H. Werner (Eds.), *The Body Percept.* New York: Random House, 1965.

Ayres, A. J. A neurobehavioral approach to evaluation and treatment of perceptual-motor dysfunction. Paper presented at the American Orthopsychiatric Association Annual Meeting, March 1967, Washington, D. C.

Ayres, A. J. Patterns of perceptual-motor dysfunction in children: A factor analytic study. *Perceptual and Motor Skills,* 1965, **20**, 335-368. (Monogr. Suppl. 1-V20.)

Balow, I. Lateral dominance characteristics and reading achievement in first grade. *Journal of Psychology,* 1963, **55**, 323-328.

Barsch, R. H. *A Movigenic Curriculum.* Bulletin No. 25, Bureau of Handicapped Children. Madison, Wis.: State Department of Public Instruction, 1965.

Belmont, L., and Birch, H. G. Lateral dominance, lateral awareness and reading disability. *Child Development,* 1965, **36**, 57-71.

Benton, A. *Right-Left Discrimination and Finger Localization.* New York: Paul B. Hoeber, 1959.

Cohen, A., and Glass, G. G. Lateral dominance in reading ability. *The Reading Teacher,* 1968, **21** (4), 343-356.

Cohen, S. A., and Berger, B. A perceptual-motor training program for early primary grade children. In S. Gordon and R. S. Colub (Eds.), *Recreation and Socialization for the Brain-Injured Child.* East Orange, N. J.: New Jersey Association for Brain-Injured Children, 1966.

Cratty, B. J. Rationale for and principles of perceptual-motor training. In G. Schiffman and D. Carter (Eds.), *Multidisciplinary Approaches to Learning Disorders.* Chicago: John Wiley, 1969.

Flick, G. L. Sinistrality revisited: A perceptual-motor approach. *Child Development,* 1966, **37** (3), 613-622.

Frostig, M., and Horne, D. *Teacher's Guide, The Frostig Program for the Development of Visual Perception.* Chicago: Follett Educational Corp., 1964.

Frostig, M., Miller, A., and Horne, D. *Teacher's Guide, Beginning Pictures and Patterns.* Chicago: Follett Educational Corp., 1966.

Frostig, M., and Horne, D. *Teacher's Guide, Intermediate Pictures and Patterns.* Chicago: Follett Educational Corp., 1966.

Frostig, M., and Horne, D. *Teacher's Guide, Advanced Pictures and Patterns.* Chicago: Follett Educational Corp., 1967.

Goodglass, H., and Quadfasel, F. A. Language laterality in left-handed aphasics. *Brain,* 1954, **77**, 521-548.

Harris, A. J. *Harris Tests of Lateral Dominance – Manual of Directions* (3rd ed.). New York: Psychological Corp., 1958.

Harris, A. J. Lateral dominance, directional confusion and reading disability. *Journal of Psychology*, 1957, **44**, 283-294.

Head, H. *Studies in Neurology.* (2 vols.). London: Oxford Univ. Press, 1920.

Hunt, J. McV. *Intelligence and Experience.* New York: Ronald Press, 1961.

Hunter, M. C. The role of physical education in child development and learning. *Journal of Health, Physical Education, and Recreation,* 1968, **39** (5), 56-58.

Ilg, F., and Ames, L. *School Readiness.* New York: Harper & Row, 1965.

Isom, J. An interpretation of dyslexia – A medical viewpoint. In G. D. Spache (Ed), *Reading Disability and Perception.* Newark, Del.: International Reading Association, 1969.

Johnson, W. Some psychological aspects of physical rehabilitation: Toward an organismic theory. *Journal of the Association of Physical and Mental Rehabilitation,* 1962, **16** (6), 165-168.

Johnson, D. J., and Myklebust, H. R. *Learning Disabilities – Educational Principles and Practices.* New York: Grune & Stratton, 1967.

Johnson, W. R., Fretz, B. R., and Johnson, J. A. Changes in self-concepts during a physical development program. *The Research Quarterly,* 1968, **39**, 560-565.

Kephart, N. C. *The Slow Learner in the Classroom.* Columbus, Ohio: Charles E. Merrill, 1960.

Kephart, N. C. Teaching the child with a perceptual-motor handicap. In M. Bortner (Ed.), *Evaluation and Education of Children with Brain Damage.* Springfield, Ill.: C. C. Thomas, 1968.

Nichols, J. Office management of patients with reading difficulties. *Canadian Medical Association Journal,* 1959, **81**, 356-360.

Orton, S. T. *Reading, Writing and Speech Problems in Children.* New York: W. W. Norton, 1961. (First published 1937.)

Painter, G. The effects of a rhythmic and sensory-motor activity program on perceptual motor spatial abilities of kindergarten children. *Exceptional Children,* 1966, **33**, 113-116.

Piaget, J. *The Psychology of Intelligence.* Totona, N. J.: Littlefield, Adams, 1966. (First published in French, 1947.)

Rabinovitch, R. D., Drew, A. L., DeJong, R. N., Ingram, W., and Withey, L. A research approach to reading retardation. *Neurology and Psychiatry in Childhood,* Vol. 34. Proceedings of the Association for Research in Nervous and Mental Disease. Baltimore: Williams & Wilkins, 1956.

Reinhold, M. The effect of laterality on reading and writing. *Proceedings of the Royal Society of Medicine, Section on Neurology,* 1963, **56**, 203-206.

Rudel, R. G., and Teuber, H. Discrimination of direction of line in children. *Journal of Comparative and Physiological Psychology,* 1963, **56** (5), 892-898.

Schilder, P. *The Image and Appearance of the Human Body.* Science Edition. New York: John Wiley, 1964. (First published in English, 1950.)

Silver, A. A., and Hagin, R. A. Strategies of intervention in the spectrum of defects in specific reading disability. Paper presented at the American Orthopsychiatric Association Annual Meeting, March 1967, Washington, D. C.

Trieschmann, R. B. Undifferentiated handedness and perceptual development in children with reading problems. *Perceptual and Motor Skills,* 1968, **27**, 1123-1134.

Wapner, S., and Werner, H. *Perceptual Development.* Worcester, Mass.: Clark Univ. Press, 1957.

Werner, H. *Comparative Psychology of Mental Development.* (Rev. ed.). New York: International Universities Press, 1957. (First published 1940.)

Witkin, H. A. Perception of body position and of the position of the visual field. *Psychological Monographs,* 1949, **63**, No. 7 (Whole No. 302).

Witkin, H. A. Perception of the upright when the direction of the force acting on the body is changed. *Journal of Experimental Psychology,* 1950, **40**, 93-106.

Witkin, H. A., and Asch, S. E. Studies in space orientation III: Perception of the upright in the absence of a visual field. *Journal of Experimental Psychology,* 1948, **38** (5), 603-614.

Witkin, H. A., Dyk, R. B., Faterson, H. F., Goodenough, D. R., and Karp, S. A. *Psychological Differentiation: Studies in Development.* New York: John Wiley, 1962.

Witkin, H. A., Lewis, H. B., Hertzman, M., Machover, K., Meissner, P. B., and Wapner, S. *Personality Through Perception.* New York: Harper, 1954.

Zangwill, O. L. Dyslexia in relation to cerebral dominance. In J. Money (Ed.), *Reading Disability.* Baltimore: Johns Hopkins Univ. Press, 1962.

Chapter 5

Creative Movement

In Chapter 2, we discussed the abilities that develop during the earliest phase of childhood — the sensory-motor phase. These abilities — awareness of the self, awareness of the environment, the ability to move, and the ability to manipulate and to master objects — constitute the basis for the total later development of children. Creative movement* is concerned with all these aspects of development. It involves the total child.

Importance of Creativity

Many people today feel alienated both from themselves and from the surrounding world. The mechanistic outlook and style of living of our age contribute to, if they do not cause, a sense of meaninglessness and chaotic confusion. Various remedies are sought. New cults spring up, and dangerous drugs are used by large masses of people to intensify the experiences of the self and of the stimuli outside. It is as if people, especially youth, have lost a clear perception of the world and of themselves and are trying desperate measures to regain it. To combat this emotional illness of our times, education must maintain its traditional role of clarifying ideas and ideals, mores, goals, and values.

Educators have at their disposal one other most powerful means of enhancing their pupils' awareness of themselves and of the world and of simultaneously enhancing their emotional and social development: helping them to become involved in creative activities. The experiences gained through creative activity heighten the individual's awareness of his own feelings, provide inner satisfaction and a sense of accomplishment, and give new meaning to his life.† If our troubled youth are given opportunities to experience the satisfactions of creative endeavor, they will have both the means and the incentive to become an optimally constructive force.

---

*Creative movement and movement exploration are synonymous terms, but the term creative movement has been chosen for this book.

†Smith (1962) points out that "The creative experience benefits the individual by freeing him to feel comfortable about using his body as an instrument for expression."

There is a connection between creativity and commitment. Creative, innovative individuals feel a commitment to their ideas and creations. They have a deep desire to work because they want to have a positive affect on both their own lives and on the lives of others. When creativity is stifled, awareness of others tends to lag, commitment to evaporate, and living to become sadly void.

Progoff (1963) has observed that the combined lack of creativity and commitment is basic to some of the ills of our society. "The major shortage of our culture," he writes, "remains a shortage of human resources, specifically a shortage of persons capable of sustained creative vision *together* with personal commitment." Awareness, commitment, and creativity are thus seen as interacting aspects of ourselves, and education needs to be concerned with all of them.

Unfortunately, educators have been too little concerned with both awareness and creativity. Children are often conditioned solely to perform along well-established and predictable lines. As a result, innovative effort is rare in our society and there is chronic resistance to change. It is essential, therefore, to introduce a creative element into education.

Creativity and Imagery

Various scholars have given us some understanding of how this task can be accomplished and have tried to suggest practical measures. The awareness of inner and outer reality and the ability to create and to feel a sense of commitment depend in part on the ability of a person to form images.

Images are necessary for the retrieval of memories, for planning the future, and for feeling empathy with others. Imagery codes and represents the events of the external world and stores these representations in the mind in both spatial and temporal dimensions. Without these images there is no basis for either rational problem solving or compassionate feelings.

An American research worker, Abravanel (1968), reported that some Russian scholars believe that the image regulates movement because movement *planning* depends on imagery. We agree with this formulation. Imagery transforms impulses and perceptions into plans, movement, and action. We also agree with the Russian scholars that movement planning and imagery can be taught, and in our opinion creative movement offers the most effective means of doing so because it involves both the planning of sequences and the employment of imagery.

Creative movement is thus of multiple value, for it can help in the development of a simultaneous awareness of the self and of the environment, and through promoting imagery it integrates levels of awareness, perception, memory, feeling, thought, and action. It is especially helpful for children of low socioeconomic levels,* inhibited children, children with perceptual deficits, children with learning difficulties, and mentally retarded children, all of whom are characteristically lacking in imagery.

Some support for the position that creative movement may be more helpful than any other activity for developing imagery comes from neurophysiological theory. Hebb (1968) presents a view of imagery based on his construct of cell assemblies. He also underscores the critical role of movement in both imagery and internal organization: "The motor process may have an organizing function of the percept itself and in imagery."

All movement is located in space and occurs at the point in time. (The importance of movement in experiencing and conceptualizing time and space is discussed in Chapter 9.) The image, like movement, also integrates temporal and spatial coordinates. Thus creative movement, which requires both motion and imagery, affords the highest possible degree of integration.

Creativity and Education

Awareness, imagery, commitment, and creativity and their interaction in philosophical, psychological, and neurophysiological terms are of great importance to the educator. But the educator who acknowledges their importance is still faced with the fundamental practical problem — what kind of teaching actually helps to develop creativity?

Mosston (1966) described various teaching styles, contrasting those in which children closely follow directions with those that help them to be independent. He suggested that children be helped to creativity by a step-by-step process of problem solving and guided discovery, progressing from dependence on the teacher for the problem and its solution to the point where the pupils are responsible for identifying the problem and exploring self-created alternative solutions. When a child translates his images and thoughts into plans and acts upon them, he engages in a creative act.

A number of educators, especially those concerned with preschool education, have been led to Sigel's conclusion that children from

---

*Observed by Sigel (1968) to be lacking in imagination.

lower socioeconomic groups have difficulties in imagery and problem solving. For this reason, Blank and Solomon (1968) believe that compensatory education should also be geared toward developing imagery and the translation of images into acts, planning, and problem solving, rather than merely providing enriching experiences.

History and Purposes of Creative Movement

New forms of physical education, variously termed gymnastics, movement exploration, movement education, or creative movement, have recently been introduced in public schools in the United States and England. These innovations, which are still evolving, are traceable to new forms of gymnastics that were developed in Central Europe and in the United States in the early part of this century by such educators as Laban in Germany, Dalcroze in Switzerland,* and Mensendieck in the United States.

Probably the greatest influence in English-speaking countries in this field was Rudolf von Laban. When Hitler was in power, Laban moved to England, where his influence on physical education was profound. His influence was symbolized by the substitution of the terms movement education or movement exploration for physical education — terms that Laban himself adopted in preference to the "gymnastics" he had used in Germany. The English and German teachers of movement education now exert an increasing influence in the United States.

"Free movement is the basis of all gymnastics." With that sentence, Laban introduced one of his main works, *Gymnastik und Tanz,* published in Germany in 1926. In it he held that the only essential for the gymnast was his "personal space," the space that he could reach with any part of his body. He regarded additional aids, such as music or gymnastic apparatus, as inessential adjuncts. During this period, in fact, he opposed the use of apparatus because he thought that it led to mechanization. Modern movement education in Eng-

---

*"Psychomotor education" is a term currently used in Europe to describe a form of therapeutic education that attempts to fuse the pedagogical basis of Dalcroze's teaching on the interaction of body and psyche with neuropsychiatric and developmental principles as set forth by Ajuriaguerra and Piaget. We recently became acquainted with the work of Madame Naville, formerly at the University of Geneva (cf. Naville and Ajuriaguerra, 1967). Naville defines four main groups of exercises that help a child experience his body as a medium for expressing ideas and feelings, as a reference point for experiencing space, and as a means of environmental contact: motor skills, body image and laterality, time and space organization, and control of individual and social behavior.

land and Germany, however, has reintroduced some apparatus to provide for such activities as climbing, jumping, and swinging. New equipment has also been developed, such as the stegel.*

The goals of "gymnastics" as formulated by Laban and others were far removed from those of physical education still practiced in Germany, which is called "turnen" and which has strong elements of competition and sportsmanship.† The goals of gymnastics are to embrace the total human being — his body, his feelings, and his mind. Laban (1926) regarded the self-regulation inherent in body movement and training as leading to a discipline of the mind also.

Such objectives are actually closer to the original purposes of gymnastic practices, which historically have been associated with religious rituals. They had as their goal achievement of greater unity with spiritual power (temple dances), or had been associated with ethical considerations aimed at optimizing human development (Greek gymnastics), or had involved a combination of these motives (Yoga). Whatever the ultimate goals of modern movement education, it should always be regarded as a means of helping develop and integrate the whole personality and every human ability.

Teaching Creative Movement

An effective movement education program must provide structured exercises involving all muscle groups and all attributes of movement (Chapter 12), not only as preparation for free movement, but also to prevent the muscular weaknesses, poor breathing, and circulatory disturbances that result from urban living. Structured exercises also ensure that children with weaknesses do not avoid exercises in the area of their difficulty. In addition, they provide a basic vocabulary of movement and they help children learn to follow directions. Because they require a set response, they also help the teacher detect children who perform less proficiently than their classmates, and they indicate the movement area in which a child requires additional help.

The sole use of structured, prescribed exercises tends to stifle children's creativity, robs them of pleasure, and leads to neglect of education of affectivity and of social awareness. In our view, therefore, both teacher-directed movement and creative movement should be used in all movement education sessions.

---

*The stegel, or Lind climber, as it is usually known in the United States, may be obtained from the Lind Climber Company, 807 Reba Place, Evanston, Illinois 60202.

† "Turnen" is derived from "turnier," meaning tournament.

Laban (1968) believed that the basic techniques of body movement should be learned and a repertoire of movements acquired, but *only* for the purpose of expressing the personality with greater range and imagination. Moreover, he did not suggest that creative expression should be delayed until a rich repertoire of movements was accumulated. Creative expression can find form in imaginative play long before the language of movement is mastered, despite the fact that imaginative play may be very restricted in some children.

Creative movement is based on children's natural movements — skipping, rolling, leaping, climbing. Children should be given ample opportunities to be active so that they can grow in movement skills and use their bodies freely as a means of self-expression. Dalcroze, the great teacher of movement and rhythmic education mentioned above, wrote (1930), "Early childhood is the age of improvisation, i.e., of spontaneous creation." He warned against imposing on children an adult style of movement.

Gestures and movements *express* moods and attitudes, but they also *create* moods and attitudes. The teacher should therefore encourage children to express positive feelings of strength, happiness, openness, and friendship by their movements. She should use movement activities to develop cooperation and strive to enhance growth and develop the ability to give and take freely. Expressions of negative feelings, however, such as anger and hostility, should not be repressed. Movement can be a valuable channel for such emotions.

In creative movement, children learn to make their bodies wide and tall.

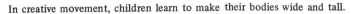

Used in this way, movement education can beneficially affect all aspects of a child's life — his work and rest, sharing and giving, and the solitary thinking necessary for understanding himself and for clarifying ideas. The anxiety, irritability, restlessness, lack of control, and preoccupation with the self that are evident in so many children (and adults) can be greatly reduced.

Even at the beginning of the program the teacher should allow each child to find his own way of solving movement problems. Let us give an example:

In a class of children with learning difficulties, one girl, Ann, was more severely handicapped in movement than the others. In fact, she had been diagnosed as having mild cerebral palsy. She had particular difficulty in releasing an object gracefully.

One child in the group wanted to dance with a colored scarf that she had brought from home. As the other children asked to join in the dance, the teacher provided scarves of different colors, and the children developed their own dance, waving the scarves in rhythmic patterns as they ran and turned, leaped, and glided. At times the children tossed their scarves in the air and caught them again.

Ann was unable to do this well — her scarf seemed to be stuck in her hands. The teacher said, "Ann, you will find your own way to do this dance." The next day Ann appeared with a doll and said, "I want to dance a mother-and-child dance because I won't have to throw my baby in the air. She can stay safely in my arms." Dancing with her doll, Ann developed a lovely sequence of movements.

The point of this example is that although some children, especially handicapped children such as Ann, need to be taught a variety of specific movements, they can at the same time engage in free movement in which the emphasis is not on conformity to the teacher's demands but on self-expression, a free flow of self-directed movement, and an individual solution to a problem. The teacher's approach ensured that Ann did not feel herself to be in competition with the other children, it helped her to sustain a good self-concept, and it enabled her to learn that to overcome her handicap she could find her own solutions to difficulties.

Directing Creative Movement

Each session of movement education, including the portion focusing on creative movement, needs to be structured, but it should never be regimented. The activities should be as child-centered as possible, the teacher posing problems that the children can solve in a variety of ways.

The children should explore various movements individually, and each child should select those that he prefers. He should learn to arrange movements in sequences. He should learn to move by himself and with a partner and in a group. As the program continues, the children should become increasingly skillful in combining movements into patterns and permitting one movement to flow imperceptibly into the next.

When the children have learned a basic movement vocabulary, including at least running, skipping, and galloping, using a ball or a hoop and such apparatus as a ladder, bar, and balance beam, a period should be set aside during which each child may choose his own activity. Later each child may try to combine several activities in a pattern at a place of his own choosing in the gym or on the playground. The teacher must be careful, however, that the children practice the activities they have set for themselves instead of playing.

To stimulate the children's inventiveness, the teacher may ask such questions as, "How else can you do that? What else can you do with the hoop or the ball? In what way can you change direction, level, or speed? How can you combine this movement with the one you did before?" In creative movement, the teacher's role is to assist and stimulate the children rather than to command.

It is most important that the children not be allowed to attempt too many things at once, and that the teacher allow ample time for reviewing what has been done. Frequent repetition is essential if children are to consolidate their gains. The children should repeat and develop elements contained in their patterns over several lessons.

Use of Space

Because free movement is concerned with the relationship of the body to space, more space is needed for creative movement than for traditional physical education programs. Space is an important cue for movement: open space invites children to move. The sight of a wet sandy beach sets them skipping; a grassy slope incites them to slide and roll, to romp, to run.

Culturally deprived children are often inhibited in free movement. They may change their attitude toward learning and toward school when guided to freely explore movement. In fact, there are children from all socioeconomic classes whose experiences have taught them to perceive the world as restricted and demanding and as one in which they are powerless. Many otherwise well-adjusted children become frightened and over-controlled in response to trauma or a strange situation. Encouragement to explore space is most beneficial.

Laban differentiates between the personal space (the sphere surrounding a person that he can touch with outstretched limbs) and the common space (the area used by the group).

It is advisable to have children reach and stretch in all directions with their arms and legs so that they can become aware of the size of their personal space while they remain stationary. But they should also move freely in the space assigned to the group, finding its dimensions through movement.

If a fairly spacious area, such as a gym or a playground, is not available, the teaching methods may have to be modified.

Grammar of Creative Movement

Both Laban and Dalcroze suggested a wide range of creative movements. Dalcroze emphasizes music and rhythm to a greater degree than Laban did. Laban emphasized body and space awareness through modification of the dimensions of movement: space, time, weight, and flow. Creative movement based on Laban's and Dalcroze's principles encourages the child to explore the boundaries of his body and its relationship to the surrounding space and to objects in space, including the bodies of other children with whom he works. It encourages them to become familiar with the feel of the body through exercises involving transfer of the weight from one part of the body to others — from the hips to the knees, to the hands, and then to the back, for example; and to become conscious of the endless possibilities of using personal and common space and objects in space creatively.

Movement follows certain laws, and Laban believed that movement could be codified in a grammar of body language. This codification makes it possible to write down a choreographic composition. It also enables the teacher to differentiate and consider an infinite variety of movements. The teacher does not need to learn Laban's notation system, but she should know Laban's practical principles, or dimensions, of movement. They will help her to understand the variety of ways in which movement sequences can be developed. (See Chapter 12 for suggestions for creative movement.)

Space

Movement sequences may be varied by changing direction in space — by moving forward, backward, sideways, and by executing different patterns on the floor, such as circles or curves or zigzags. Some children have difficulty in describing specific floor

Walking on a cord helps children learn to describe floor patterns.

patterns. For these children, it is helpful to place a cord on the floor in the desired shape and have the children walk along beside it. The cord is then removed, but the children pretend it is there and walk "beside" it in the same pattern. The children then learn to walk and run floor patterns in different directions and to proceed along them backward and sideways as well as forward. Different movements, patterns, and directions may be combined. For example, the children may run forward in a wavy line and then walk straight backward, or they may walk in a zigzag line and then hop in a circle.

Space also has a vertical direction, and movement may be extended upward by stretching, jumping, and leaping; or it may be compressed by using a bent position or by crouching, rolling, or curling up on the floor. Different parts of the body may move in various directions simultaneously. For example, a child may jump forward while his arms are flung out to the sides and the trunk is bent backward.

Time

The element of time (changes in speed) can be combined with the other dimensions, the children consciously making their movements slow or fast, sudden or sustained, accelerating or decelerating. The rhythm of the movements may also be made even or uneven.

Flow

Another dimension of movement is its flow. Laban discriminates between bound movements and free flowing movements. Bound movements are those that can be immediately controlled, stopped, or changed. They are necessary in negotiating an obstacle course and in sports in which sudden changes in speed or direction are required. In free flowing movements, tight controls are absent. The movement may follow its course unaffected by external forces until it gradually terminates, perhaps with a gentle sinking to the ground and total relaxation. Or a movement may accelerate until it reaches an apogee and necessarily comes to an end.

A flowing movement may be limited to a specific body part, as in swinging an arm, or it may involve the whole body at once, or it may involve different parts of the body successively, as in bowling or throwing a discus.

The children may experiment with flowing movements in which some body parts lead and the others follow. They can, for instance, learn that a movement may originate in the center of the body and spread outward, such as changing from a coiled position to a horizontal stretch position. Or they can learn that a movement can begin at the periphery and pull the rest of the body after it, as when a leg is swung out and the weight of the body follows. The children may also experiment with interrupting a flow of movement with a sudden controlled movement, such as landing perfectly still after a jump.

Weight

The dimension of weight may be changed by adjusting muscle tension to emphasize or de-emphasize movements so that heavy, forceful movement may be contrasted with light, gentle movement.

Gravity

Movements may also be varied in regard to the part of the body that is supported (Laban, 1968). For example, movements may be executed lying down, standing, sitting, kneeling, squatting, or standing on tiptoe on one foot. A child may explore gravity by having his

body supported on one point only, as when hopping on one foot;
he may use four points, as in crawling on hands and knees; or he
may use three points, as in sitting on the floor and propelling himself about with his hands. A movement may change from one point
of support to another point, such as changing from a standing position to sitting with the legs in the air or to kneeling with hands on
the floor.

Shape

The teacher needs to consider the position of the body at the beginning of a movement sequence, during a movement sequence, and
at the end of a movement sequence. The initial position of a movement involving jumping, for example, might be a crouch position,
or an upright position with one foot in front of the other, or a running position that leads into the first jump. During a movement
sequence, a child might try to make his body tall, occupying as little
space sideways as possible as if he were an arrow; or his position
might be spread out or curled up as if he were a ball; or twisted as
if he were a screw. At the end of a movement sequence, he might
be in a standing position with feet apart, or crouched, or preparing
to run. A part of the body, rather than the whole body, may also
change position during a movement sequence, as when a child swings
his arms sideways while jumping or turns his head and shoulders
while stepping backward.

Level

The level of the body may also be varied during movement. The
children may make floor patterns close to the floor (crawling, creep-
ing, crouching, rolling, scooting, crab-walking, for instance); at the
normal walking level; or at a high level (on tiptoe, stretching, and
leaping, for instance). When the children have done movement sequences at each level, it may be suggested that they change from
one level to another during a sequence.

Air Patterns

The children should become aware of the patterns their bodies make
in the air as they bend, stretch, twist, and swing their arms and legs.
They should try to make air patterns while standing in one place
and later combine them with floor patterns.

Making an air pattern differs from merely assuming a position or
exploring space with arms or legs because the air pattern is made up
of continuous movements creating a discernible pattern. The pattern

Walking on all fours on discs is a feat of balance.

may be symmetrical, as when a child describes large horizontal or vertical circles with both arms. Or it may be asymmetrical, as when he stands on one foot and slowly bends forward and backward while weaving varieties of shapes in the air with his head and one arm.

Movement Variations in Several Dimensions

Movement may be varied in several dimensions simultaneously. For example, fast walking may be changed to slow rolling; skipping may be changed to standing still and swinging the arms in various directions. Change in one dimension of movement usually necessitates changes in other dimensions.

Laban and Lawrence (1947) said, " . . . the central problem in achieving efficient movement is in our opinion the development and safeguarding of the sense of proportions of the factors of motion, weight, space, and time, and their controlled flow."

Movement in Groups and Pairs

The children should not be aware of only the movements of their own bodies. When they act as a group — running, jumping, skipping, or walking various paths — they also need to be aware of each other so that they are able either to react to or interact with each other. Avoiding each other, meeting each other, moving against each other, leading, following, observing, imitating, supporting each other – all lead to new movement ideas and sequences.

Complexity of interaction should, however, be reached by degrees. After working alone sufficiently to become acquainted with his own body and the movements he can perform, a child may undertake simple group activities that do not require close cooperation, such as moving around a group or in contrast to a group, or walking forward or backward or running patterns with other children, taking care to avoid collisions.

Of intermediate difficulty is working in pairs, which should be practiced before the more complicated group activities. The children might first walk about in pairs holding hands and then learn to skip together. Then they may move on to more complicated activities, such as forming a wheelbarrow – one child walking forward on his hands, body roughly parallel to the ground, while the other walks behind supporting him by the ankles. Advanced children may perform reciprocal movements in which one child adjusts the shape of his body to the other; or they may match the shapes of their bodies during movement sequences, one child copying the other.

Examples of group activities that require a great deal of cooperation and are therefore difficult to achieve are creative dancing and twisting in and out of spaces formed by the body of another child.

This 12-foot tower is a popular piece of playground equipment.

The children should also learn to avoid or to overcome obstacles
– to get around, under, and over objects – without interrupting the
free flow of movement.

Mimetic Play

By stimulating the imagination, mimetic play provides excellent cues
for creative movement. A child may pretend to be a giant walking
slowly on a rough road or stomping along in anger. Or he may imitate the gait of an old woman, pretend to fly like a bird, pull a
heavy cart, or chase a wind-blown balloon. In each case, different
kinds of movement are evoked, and the child experiences different
feelings. Mimetic play results in longer movement phrasing, which
stimulates concentration and the development of movement ideas
into independent playlets or dances, thereby fulfilling the need for
creative expression through movement.

Mimetic cues may be used with young children in every session,
but not more than twice, and only then for short periods because
children also need to become aware of themselves as they really are.
The teacher must also remember that her aim is to stimulate a certain kind of movement – to induce a realistic portrayal of a person
or thing. She should not say, therefore, "Imitate a fairy," but instead, "Run lightly as a fairy who barely touches the ground." And
she should not say, "Move as a flower," but instead, "Grow and
stretch toward the light as a flower opening its petals." Later the
teacher can frequently omit the similes and instruct the children
simply to produce the movement she desires – leaping, galloping,
bending, stretching, turning, gliding, thrusting, or striding – only
occasionally using mimetic games because they contribute to the enjoyment of the children.

Works Cited

Abravenel, E. The development of intersensory patterning with regard to selected spatial dimensions. *Monograph of the Society for
Research in Child Development,* 1968, **33** (2), Serial No. 118.

Blank, M., and Solomon, F. A tutorial language program to develop
abstract thinking in socially disadvantaged preschool children.
Child Development, 1968, **39** (2), 379-389.

Dalcroze, A. J. *Eurythmics, Art, and Education.* F. Rothwell
(Trans.). London: Chatto and Windus, 1930.

Hebb, D. O. Concerning imagery. *Psychological Review,* 1968,
75, 466-477.

Laban, R. *Gymnastik und Tanz.* Oldenburg, Germany: Gerhard Stalling, Verlag, 1926.

Laban, R. *Modern Educational Dance.* (2nd rev. ed.) New York: Praeger, 1968. (First published 1948.)

Laban, R., and Lawrence, F. C. *Effort.* London: MacDonald & Evans, 1947.

Mosston, M. *Teaching Physical Education.* Columbus, Ohio: Charles E. Merrill, 1966.

Naville, S., and Ajuriaguerra, J. H. Rééducation psychomotrice. *Revue Belge de Therapeutique Physique,* 1967, **34,** 3-14.

Progoff, I. *The Symbolic and the Real.* New York: Julian Press, 1963.

Sigel, I. Contributions of Piagetian theory to research on preschool environments. Paper presented at the 1968 annual meeting of the American Psychological Association, San Francisco.

Smith, H. M. Creative expression and physical education. *Journal of Health, Physical Education, and Recreation,* 1962, **33** (5), 38-39.

Developing Psychological Functions Through Movement Education

In Chapter 1 it was said that the central goals of movement education are the development of movement skills, the deepening of body awareness, and the promotion of health and a feeling of well-being. It should be reiterated that movement is a necessity for both adequate physical and healthy psychological development, but crowded urban conditions and modern conveniences often permit little opportunity for children to move about freely.

Because movement education can provide a partial substitute for this loss, a daily exercise period would be warranted if only for the purpose of promoting good health and developing children's sensory-motor abilities. Movement education, however, can be so directed that it will simultaneously enhance other developmental abilities.

In Chapter 2 the developmental sequence was discussed, and a description was given of the abilities that enable children to master and respond to their environment. All of these abilities — sensory-motor, language, perception, higher cognitive functioning, and emotional and social development — should be taken into account in all school teaching, including movement education.

In this chapter a discussion of the influence of movement education on various psychological functions is presented and methods are outlined for integrating training of these abilities with the main goals of movement education.* The regulatory functions of the nervous system, which modify the global aspects of behavior (Chapter 1), must also be considered.

---

*Singer's text (1968a) provides an excellent summary of the psychological factors that affect the acquisition of motor skills. Cratty's book (1968) uses the findings of many areas of behavioral research relevant to the teaching and coaching of physical activities. The teacher will find these are valuable sources. They are, however, focused on improvement of motor skills per se; they are not primarily concerned with the effect of movement education on other psychological functions nor do they center on the elementary school years.

Language Development

Many children entering school have difficulty in understanding and using language. John (1963) and Deutsch (1964) have commented on this disability in culturally deprived children; and Drowatsky (1965) has noted it in children diagnosed as brain damaged. Nearly 40 percent of children referred to the Children's Physical Development Clinic of the University of Maryland because of faulty neuromuscular control or other developmental problems evidenced some type of speech problem (Johnson and Hendricks, 1965). But language difficulties, far from being restricted to special groups, may be found in any classroom.

The Illinois Test of Psycholinguistic Abilities (McCarthy and Kirk, 1961; McCarthy and Kirk, 1963; Kirk, McCarthy, and Kirk, 1968), based on Osgood's (1957) model of the communication process, is widely used to explore various aspects of a child's language development. This test was designed to provide a basis for constructing individualized training programs to ameliorate specific weaknesses and to guide the choice of teaching methods from knowledge of a child's specific strengths. For educational purposes, the authors have found it helpful to categorize the abilities explored by the ITPA into receptive, expressive, memory, and associative functions. Movement education can influence all these functions. When working with children who show lags in their language development, as, for instance, the culturally deprived child, the slow learning child, and the neurologically handicapped child, the teacher can emphasize those methods and procedures that are most likely to promote mastery of language.

Receptive Language

Many children have difficulty in following directions, especially when the directions are not addressed to them individually but to the whole group. The teacher may be unaware that a child has failed to understand her and may only discover his lack of comprehension when the child attempts an incorrect assignment or does the correct assignment incorrectly. Such errors are sometimes due to difficulty in maintaining attention, but often even with the utmost attentiveness the child does not understand the teacher's directions.

Teaching children to follow directions is a natural part of movement education, because the children's movements usually occur in response to the teacher's verbal directions. As the children respond with overt movements, the teacher can see at once that a child does not respond correctly and can find out if he misunderstood the directions. She then can help with additional explanation. A child can also become aware of his own errors and those of others by observing the movements of the rest of the group and correct for himself his misperception of the teacher's directions.

To avoid being misunderstood, the teacher should begin with simple, short directions, making them gradually longer and more complex as the children's abilities to attend and to comprehend increase. The teacher can also enlarge the children's vocabularies by slowly introducing new words and taking care to repeat and explain them.

In the early school years, children often have difficulty in learning to understand and use appropriately words that denote points in time and space or the relationship between points in time and space. Examples of such words are *around, sideways, intersecting, before, after, in between, in front, backward, crossover,* and *forward.*

A child who can understand simple statements about single isolated events, such as "John plays," "The girl laughs," or "This is a tree," will not necessarily be able to comprehend statements denoting relationships in time and space, such as "The girls laughed after they saw the clown," "John played with the big ball before putting the small one in the basket," "The tree behind that bush stands between the house and the street."

Children can learn to understand and to react to directions denoting relationships in time and space during movement education. A two-step direction can be fused into one as time progresses and the children learn to understand more complicated directions. For instance, "Put the ball in front of the rope. Now step over the rope" can later become "After putting the ball in front of the rope, step over the rope."

Words denoting comparison are also difficult because they describe relationships. Examples of comparatives that refer to time and space are *slower, faster, sooner, later, wider, smaller, higher,* and *lower.*

Movement education can provide children with a vocabulary denoting time and space relations and with the concepts represented by these words because movement always has temporal and spatial extensions. The teacher should introduce the words systematically, using the various exercises to illustrate events and relationships in time and space.

Another difficulty in understanding spoken language does not derive from lack of knowledge of words and concepts but from difficulty in grasping two or more ideas that describe aspects of one movement. A child may understand "Take two steps," or "Go forward," but be baffled by "Take two steps forward."

Other children may be able to comprehend " Take two steps forward" but not a sequence of directions, such as "Take two steps forward, make a half-turn so that you face the window, and then take two steps backward." Practice can be given in following such simple sequences, and when the children are proficient, sequential directions of greater complexity can be given.

Memory for sequences, as well as the attributes of movement, can be trained with the help of markings on the playground or floor.* A series of straight lines, enclosed shapes, and zigzags helps children acquire the memory for two, three, or more consecutive movements. The markings should be about two feet apart — far enough to be distinct but not too far for the children to jump from one to another. Cratty suggests that control of a group of children is aided if the markings are roughly in a semicircle so that the children finish a sequence fairly close to the position from which they started. The following is an example:

A child must remember a complex sequence of directions for the markings below because lines and shapes other than those named in the directions are nearby. He thus receives practice in figure-ground perception as well as sequencing. A child might be asked to "Jump into the little circle, walk along the bottom straight line, jump into the first dot at the end of the line, and finally run along the zigzag line."

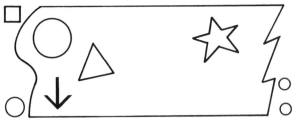

*Figures may be formed with removable discs, rods, dowels, or ropes to avoid permanent markings, which may become confusing (see Chapter 10).

For the markings below, the sequence of figures is simple and clear, but the child must remember directions for a more complex sequence of movements than he did previously.

He might be asked to "Walk right on the straight line. Try not to put a foot down outside it. When you get to the end of the straight line, jump into the triangle with your feet apart and your arms in the air. Next hop into the square on your left foot, and then jump into the circle, turning in the air as you jump." The child practices balance, agility, strength, right-left discrimination, and form recognition.

Memory for sequences can also be trained during movement education without special markings by giving such instructions as, "Walk to the ladder, turn around, hop three times, and then run back to the starting point." But the markings help children to form a mental image — a map of the spatial aspects of their surroundings — and to visualize and remember spatial relationships.

Body awareness can be enhanced greatly if a child is told to contact a certain marked off spot on the ground with various parts of his body. He can, for instance, be told to put one elbow on a disc, put one knee into a triangle, put his right heel on a dowel, or put one foot into one of the loops of the figure 8 and the other foot into the other loop.

Clinical experience shows that if directions for exercises are first given at the level at which the children can comprehend, and then are gradually lengthened, the span of attention can be extended, together with the necessary ability to visualize, memorize, and plan.

If the teacher consciously and deliberately frames her directions for the purpose, movement education can be an excellent vehicle for furthering receptive language skills, increasing children's auditory memory span, developing vocabulary and concepts, and training the ability to keep several ideas in mind simultaneously (see section on higher cognitive functions) without in any way compromising the objectives of enhancing physical development, movement skills, and body awareness.

Expressive Language

It is less easy to integrate expressive language into movement education than to integrate receptive language. If children are encouraged to use language too extensively in movement education, the tempo of the program may be retarded. Caution is therefore necessary. But expressive language can nevertheless be improved within the framework of movement education as it is conducted in regular classes, and it should certainly be emphasized with children who suffer from specific difficulties in language or in thought processes. Such children should be asked to repeat directions, tell about the exercise they are going to do or the game they are going to play, describe it afterwards, and after mimetic activities explain the meaning of their actions and gestures.

The teacher should aim at teaching children to use spoken language in planning, discussing, carrying out, and evaluating movement sequences. They should give directions themselves. They should take turns at being "teacher." A child who needs help with expressive language should be asked to describe aloud the movements or sequence he is about to undertake, tell about the movements as he performs them, and subsequently describe and discuss what he did. The same sequence should then be undertaken to the accompaniment of unspoken, inner language (thought) and be repeated until the sequence becomes automatic (Luria, 1961).

The importance of language in learning tasks, including motor tasks, is shown by Rieber (1968). When a child is able to use verbal mediation (to express in language what he is to do), he can accomplish a new task immediately. If verbal mediation cannot be or is not employed, however, the child may learn the task only gradually. Verbal mediation is a most efficient method of learning most tasks.

A film seen several years ago illustrated this fact directly and humorously. A truck driver was being taught to dance by his girl friend, but he seemed an utter failure. But when he said, "Okay, right foot is the gas, left foot is the clutch," he performed the dance sequence perfectly: "Step on the gas, tap the brake, advance the clutch smoothly, and step hard on the gas."

Training in language and verbal mediation will necessitate a certain amount of adaptation in conducting the exercises, since the directions to the children and some of their reactions will differ to some degree from the usual directions and reactions. The nature of the physical exercise will not change, however. Even when language training is involved, it is important that the teacher try to maintain a brisk pace in conducting the movement education program. (See Chapter 9, where the importance of movement without verbalization is discussed. Movement with and without verbalization should be used.)

Visual Perception

Some physical education programs are part of more general visual-motor programs that have training in visual perception as a major goal. Programs of this type include those by Kephart (1960), Getman (1962), and Barsch (1965). Kephart, Getman, and Barsch each combine visual perceptual training, such as tracing or recognition of shapes, with motor training.

In our program, movement training is differentiated from visual perception. Movement and perception are regarded as different functions. The human organism can respond to the environment either by perceiving it or by reacting to it with overt movement, which usually involves skeletal adjustment. It is quite possible to recognize and discriminate visual stimuli without any movement except the minimal movement of the eye itself. It is equally possible for movement to occur without perception of the world outside and even without consciousness, as during sleep. Of course, movement and perception are usually integrated, as in the visual-motor act of threading a needle. Movement depends upon perception and usually occurs as a result of it, but it is not perception itself. We can perceive a pencil on the desk without any overt movement; we can guide it visually when writing.

For this reason, the visual perception training programs developed at the Frostig Center of Educational Therapy (1964, 1966-1967) and this movement education program are published as separate entities. The visual perception programs do, however, include suggestions for physical exercises that are essential as an adjunct to visual perceptual training. In this textbook, development of movement skills is the primary focus. Separate training focusing on perception is therefore recommended. Each program focuses on a different developmental ability, and each is designed to supplement the other, both for general training in the primary grades and for remedial work.

Movement education exercises, including a great variety of activities requiring visual-motor coordination and transfer, help children improve specific visual perceptual skills, such as perception of distance, the position of the body in relation to the environment, spatial relationships, and sequencing. Activities that develop visual perceptual and other developmental abilities are, for instance, avoiding obstacles, throwing and catching, and imitating movements or movement sequences (which may be demonstrated by the teacher or with pictures). Such activities are especially helpful, as are those that require a child to respond to visual cues provided by other children. Visual-motor coordination is also enhanced by the exercises mentioned on pages 86 and 87.

In Chapters 4 and 5 exercises are described that have been designated to promote kinesthetic perception specifically, and suggestions are given for developing body awareness, directionality, and laterality, all of which influence visual perception. It should be reemphasized, however, that a movement education program cannot substitute for a comprehensive training program in visual perception, either in the regular classroom or for remedial purposes.

Imagery

The term visualization is often used for all imagery because with most people visual mental images serve memory more frequently than do auditory images or images of smell, taste, or touch.*   In common language there are not even words corresponding to visualization to designate imagery pertaining to the other senses.

Visualization depends upon visual perceptual experiences, and it is essential not only for memory but also for thought processes. The ability to visualize – use imagery – is crucial because it is basic to mental manipulation and abstraction and therefore to the understanding of what is not present.

Kohler (1959) observed that chimpanzees possess a primitive language and can learn to understand some elements of a "foreign" language – the human one. But Kohler points out that because animals are very limited in their ability to use mental imagery, their repertoire is restricted and painfully acquired. Only a few animals can use tools, such as a stick to dig with or to push something about. The solution of problems, he states, including the invention and use of tools, depends upon imagery, and this attribute, which makes motor planning possible, is essentially human.

Imagery can be developed during movement education through planning movement sequences (as discussed in Chapter 5), through problem solving methods, such as those used by Mosston (1965, 1966) and Laban (1968), through executing memory sequences as mentioned above, and through the use of mimetic and dramatic activities.

---

*Luria (1968), however, describes how memory traces of multisensory experiences are fused into images to make possible extraordinary feats of memory.

Auditory Perception

Many books and articles have been written about the role of vision in physical education, but auditory perception and the integration of auditory and motor functions are rarely discussed. Auditory perception is trained when children attend to verbal directions or when they translate music into movement in dance and rhythm exercises. These activities also involve the simultaneous integration of kinesthetic and visual perception in the total experience; thus they are particularly valuable in promoting intersensory integration.

The use of musical and percussion instruments also helps develop children's perception of tone, loudness, rhythm, and musical sequence, and it stimulates children to movement. Nevertheless, care should be taken not to use musical instruments excessively, for children should also become aware of their own rhythm, style, and speed of movement.

Additional training for auditory perception can be conducted during rest periods between physical exercises. Montessori (1965) introduced listening exercises during which the children were blindfolded. These exercises are valuable. The teacher may simply make a succession of sounds by clapping, hitting blocks together, ringing a bell, or crumpling paper and ask the children what sounds they heard. (Children who do not like to be blindfolded may close their eyes or cover them with their hands.) The teacher may also have the children sit in a circle and react to the sounds. For example, they may lower their heads when they hear a very deep sound, raise them when they hear a medium sound, and slowly stretch their hands up high when they hear a very high sound.

These exercises must be short or they become boring, but they are much more soothing than the conventional rest period, which many children dislike.

Higher Cognitive Functions

The phrase higher cognitive functions refers to the sum total of the ways in which a human being becomes aware of and obtains knowledge about the outside world without direct involvement of his sense organs. Perceptual processes register only the here and now — the stimuli immediately available to the senses, such as the smell of a lemon, the touch of a hand, the sound of a melody, or the sight of a picture. Higher cognitive functions (or thought processes, to use a more familiar term), such as imagery, memory, judgment, critical evaluation, and problem solving, can be concerned with what is not immediately present and exposed to the senses.

Distinctions among psychological functions are rarely clear-cut; psychological functions blend into each other without sharp dividing lines. Thus the higher cognitive functions enumerated previously may be categorized in various other ways. Because associative processes and memory functions are involved in perception, in language, and in thought processes, they can be discussed in all of these various contexts. In this discussion, however, we consider memory and associations as higher cognitive functions.

Transfer of Training

The questions then are: Are higher cognitive functions involved in movement education? Can gains be made in these functions within the framework of movement education? If so, will they be transferred to other activities and to the development of cognitive processes in general?

Research results concerning the effectiveness of training and the amount of transfer of gains to any other contexts or situations are meager and sometimes contradictory. For instance, Oliver (1958) found that a group of educable mentally retarded boys given a special physical education program for ten weeks gained 25 percent in IQ scores. Oliver attributes this gain to the effect of achievement and success, improved adjustment, physical fitness, and a feeling of importance. An example of a study reporting a high relationship between motor skills (motor coordination and balance tasks) and intellectual achievement is that of Ismail, Kephart, and Cowell (1963). A factor analytic study reported by Ismail, Kane, and Kirdendall (1969) showed that intelligence items loaded on the same factor as coordination and some balance items. Plack (1968) found generally positive relationships between reading and motor skill abilities. Singer (1968a), on the other hand, found low and generally nonsignificant correlations.

Clinical experience, however, indicates that children who learn during movement education to keep several directions in mind at once will probably be able to follow multiple directions in the classroom also. Children who learn to plan a sequence of actions during movement education will probably learn to plan and execute the steps in a science experiment faster than children who have not had this kind of preparation. Children who learn to find solutions to a movement problem during movement education (see Chapter 5) may be expected to be more ready to look for solutions in other situations, to put sequential events in order, to keep several ideas in mind simultaneously, to search for new patterns, to recognize a problem.

Cognitive functions are influenced by culture. There is no doubt that the subculture that is the school itself influences cognitive functions. How great this influence is probably depends upon the school's success in getting children into the habit of solving problems. Bruner (1966), Torrance (1965), Suchman (1962), Cope (1967), and others have shown the great value of a problem-solving approach to education.

Concept Formation

Since concept formation is often regarded as the basis of all intellectual activity, the role of movement education in helping develop concept formation is important.

Concepts develop with accumulated experience, which contributes to the categories in which we classify our experiences. Concepts change and become enriched as new experiences are added. Children who have seen a swan, a magpie, a parrot, an eagle, pigeons, and sparrows have richer concepts of what a bird is than children who have seen pigeons and sparrows. The words we use to label concepts delineate them and distinguish them from other concepts. Children learn to differentiate between birds and non-birds as they hear the label of bird applied correctly and frequently.

As children acquire new concepts, they associate them with those they have formed previously. They perceive new relationships and form higher order concepts. Thus words are used to help establish concepts and relationships between concepts, to group them, to organize them, and to establish hierarchies of concepts.

Many concepts used in movement education require a high level of abstraction. The concepts of time and space and of force and resistance, which are involved in such concepts as speed, weight, and balance, can only be acquired through a process of enrichment based upon successive experiences.

Creative movement (Chapter 5) is especially helpful in building higher order concepts because part of the educational method requires the conscious modification of movement in regard to the dimensions of time and space, of force and resistance.

By experiencing movement and talking about their actions, children acquire ideas of how to use movements and verbal expressions for their movement experiences. In addition to these general concepts, the movement education program engenders more specific concepts pertaining to body structure and function, health, and social behavior. Mimetic and dramatic activities can be particularly effective in providing concepts pertaining to all aspects of children's lives, as well as concepts pertaining to social studies and other fields of knowledge.

Concepts of Intelligence

Binet and Simon (1916) considered three broad characteristics of intelligence: (1) following directions; (2) maintaining a purpose; and (3) critical evaluation.

Following directions is a pervasive element of the movement education program. Maintaining a purpose is practiced when children have to keep multiple directions in mind, as when they reproduce a sequence of movements or execute a complicated movement or position that has been described to them.

It is easier for children to combine whole movements into a temporal sequence than to combine part movements into a complex whole, so whole movements should be practiced first. Examples have been given earlier in this chapter (see page 85 and see also page 86). The sequences should gradually become more complex. Translating complex directions into movement sequences gives practice not only in maintaining a purpose but also in using visual imagery and keeping each part of the series of directions in mind while carrying out the whole sequence.

The same is true of achieving a single complex body position by keeping in mind and coordinating the directions for several simultaneous part movements. An example is when the children are asked to "Stand with feet slightly apart, toes turned slightly outward, weight mostly on the left foot, left knee slightly bent, and right knee straight." If the arm positions are included, the directions become even more complex. For instance: "The right arm is to be held straight up above the head; left arm in front of the body, parallel to the floor." The teacher needs to begin with very simple directions and make them more and more complex. A simpler example is given on page 85 of this chapter.

Binet's and Simon's third attribute of intelligence — critical evaluation — may be developed if children are given opportunities to discuss their performances of exercises and of mimetic and dramatic activities. Some educators, such as Mosston (1965, 1966), emphasize evaluation of the children's activities by the children themselves as an integral part of all physical education. In the present program it is particularly emphasized during creative movement (Chapter 5).

After two-thrids of a century, Binet's and Simon's characteristics of intelligence are still valid, and they are used here for the sake of simplicity. Much more detailed and scientific analyses of intellectual functions have appeared since their time – those of Spearman (1927), Wechsler (1958), and Guilford (1967), to name but a few. It would, however, take us far out of our way to discuss these models in the context of the movement education program.

Works Cited

Barsch, R. H. *A Movigenic Curriculum.* Bulletin No. 25, Bureau of Handicapped Children. Madison, Wis.: State Department of Public Instruction, 1965.

Binet, A., and Simon, T. *The Development of Intelligence in Children.* Baltimore: Williams & Wilkins, 1916.

Bruner, J. S. *Toward a Theory of Instruction.* Cambridge, Mass.: Harvard Univ. Press, 1966.

Cope, J. *Discovery Methods in Physical Education.* London: Thomas Nelson and Sons, 1967.

Cratty, B. J. *Psychology and Physical Activity.* Englewood Cliffs, N.J.: Prentice-Hall, 1968.

Deutsch, M. Facilitating development in the preschool child: Social and psychological perspectives. *Merrill-Palmer Quarterly*, 1964, **10**, 249-263.

Drowatsky, J. Physical education for the brain-damaged child. *Physical Educator,* 1965, **2** (2), 76-77.

Frostig, M., and Horne, D. *Teacher's Guide, The Frostig Program for the Development of Visual Perception.* Chicago: Follett Educational Corp., 1964.

Frostig, M., Miller, A., and Horne, D. *Teacher's Guide, Beginning Pictures and Patterns.* Chicago: Follett Educational Corp., 1966.

Frostig, M., and Horne, D. *Teacher's Guide, Intermediate Pictures and Patterns.* Chicago: Follett Educational Corp., 1966.

Frostig, M., and Horne, D. *Teacher's Guide, Advanced Pictures and Patterns.* Chicago: Follett Educational Corp., 1967.

Getman, G. N. *How to Develop Your Child's Intelligence.* Luverne, Minn.: Author, 1962.

Guilford, J. P. *The Nature of Human Intelligence.* New York: McGraw-Hill, 1967.

Ismail, A. H., Kane, J., and Kirdendall, D. R. Relationships among intellectual and nonintellectual variables. *The Research Quarterly,* 1969, **40**, 83-92.

Ismail, A. H., Kephart, N.C., and Cowell, C. C. Utilization of motor aptitude tests in predicting academic achievement. Technical Report No. 1. Purdue Univ. Research Foundation, P.U. 879-64-838. Lafayette, Ind.: 1963.

John, V. P. The intellectual development of slum children: Some preliminary findings. *American Journal of Orthopsychiatry,* 1963, **33**, 813-822.

Johnson, W. R., and Hendricks, R. Management of speech handicaps in clinical physical education. *Journal of the Association for Physical and Mental Rehabilitation,* 1965, **19 (2)**, 45-46.

Kephart, N. C. *The Slow Learner in the Classroom.* Columbus, Ohio: Charles E. Merrill, 1960.

Kirk, S. A., McCarthy, J., and Kirk, W. *The Illinois Test of Psycholinguistic Abilities.* (Rev. ed.). Urbana: Univ. of Illinois Press, 1968.

Kohler, W. *The Mentality of Apes.* New York: Vintage, 1959. (First published 1927.)

Laban, R. *Modern Educational Dance.* (2nd rev. ed.). New York: Praeger, 1968. (First published 1948.)

Luria, A. R. *The Mind of a Mnemonist — A Little Book About a Vast Memory.* New York: Basic Books, 1968.

'Luria, A. R. *The Role of Speech in the Regulation of Normal and Abnormal Behavior.* New York: Liveright, 1961.

McCarthy, J., and Kirk, S. A. *The Construction, Standardization, and Statistical Characteristics of the Illinois Test of Psycholinguistic Abilities.* Urbana: Univ. of Illinois Press, 1963.

McCarthy, J., and Kirk, S. A. *The Illinois Test of Psycholinguistic Abilities.* Urbana: Univ. of Illinois Press, 1961.

Montessori, M. *Dr. Montessori's Own Handbook.* New York: Schocken Books, 1965.

Mosston, M. *Developmental Movement.* Columbus, Ohio: Charles E. Merrill, 1965.

Mosston, M. *Teaching Physical Education.* Columbus, Ohio: Charles E. Merrill, 1966.

Oliver, J. N. The effect of physical conditioning exercises and activities on the mental characteristics of educationally sub-normal boys. *British Journal of Educational Psychology,* 1958, **28**, 155-165.

Osgood, C. E. A behavioristic analysis. In J. Bruner (Ed.), *Contemporary Approaches to Cognition.* Cambridge, Mass.: Harvard Univ. Press, 1957.

Plack, J. J. Relationship between achievement in reading and achievement in selected motor skills in elementary school children. *The Research Quarterly,* 1968, **39**, 1063-1068.

Rieber, M. Mediational aids and motor skill learning in children. *Child Development*, 1968, **39** (2), 559-567.

Singer, R. N. Interrelationship of physical, perceptual-motor, and academic achievement variables in elementary school children. *Perceptual and Motor Skills*, 1968a, **27**, 1323-1332.

Singer, R. N. *Motor Learning and Human Performance: An Application to Physical Education Skills.* New York: Macmillan, 1968b.

Spearman, C. *The Abilities of Man.* London: Macmillan, 1927.

Suchman, J. R. *The Elementary School Training Program in Scientific Inquiry.* Urbana: Univ. of Illinois Press, 1962.

Torrance, E. P. *Rewarding Creative Behavior: Experiments in Classroom Creativity.* Englewood Cliffs, N.J.: Prentice-Hall, 1965.

Wechsler, D. *The Measurement and Appraisal of Adult Intelligence.* (4th ed.). Baltimore: Williams & Wilkins, 1958.

Chapter 7

Associative Processes

Human beings, and even animals, must exercise various abilities simultaneously in order to survive. They may need to look, to listen, to touch, to vocalize, to move — all at the same time.

Mother puts the meat in the oven. She uses her eyes to guide her hands; she feels the heat from the oven and avoids burning herself. At the same time, she hears the phone ring. She listens for the baby's cry and hurries to answer the phone lest it awaken him. In so doing, she has had to connect, to understand, and to differentiate the various sensory impressions, and she has had to react to several of them simultaneously and successively in a discriminating fashion.

In everyday life, the ability of the human brain to receive a large amount of widely varied information and to react to it immediately, selectively, and appropriately is so common that it is taken for granted. Many of the associations needed in performing complex acts have passed the level of conscious performance and have become automatic as a result of continual experience and practice.

The example above illustrates the abilities of the human being to (1) select sensory stimuli from his environment and associate them with each other; (2) integrate perceptions so that they form a coherent and uniform picture of the world; (3) integrate these perceptions with the memories of former experiences; and (4) respond in adaptive fashion.

It is important to understand that there are three major groups of associative processes: (1) associating perceptions (input) with responses (output); (2) integrating* perceptions (input) from two or more sense organs; and (3) associating present stimuli with earlier experiences. All depend upon previous experiences, and all are functions of the central nervous system.

---

*English and English (1958) define *association* as "a functional relationship between psychological phenomena established in the course of individual experience and of such nature that the presence of one tends to evoke the other; . . ." They define *integration* as "the process . . . of bringing together and unifying parts into a whole; . . . It is a stronger term than *association, coordination,* or *organization.* In integration, though the parts may be distinguished, they lose their separate identity."

Development of Associative Processes

Various constructs have been postulated as necessary for associative processes, ranging from images (Bruner, 1966; Hebb, 1959, 1968) and schemata (Piaget, 1967) to anatomical changes (Krech, 1962), but all theorists emphasize that the ability to associate is a result of interaction between the person and his environment.

Almost from birth, children learn to associate movement responses with the stimuli they receive through their different sense organs. A three-month-old baby, who was observed immediately before feeding, pursed his lips and made sucking movements as the bottle was lowered to his mouth. A spoon brought near his face made him open his mouth wide. Sensory stimuli, probably tactile and olfactory as well as visual, were already associated with movement responses.*

Intersensory associations are also formed very early. They are the basis of children's ability to recognize an object or event regardless of the sense organ through which it is presented. An infant first becomes aware of the touch and smell of his mother; later he can recognize her by sight and by the sound of her footsteps.

The ability to integrate the input of different sense organs is an important aspect of growth in recognizing and knowing the world around us. A stimulus received through one sense organ may evoke memories of perceptions received previously through other organs. When we see a picture of a brook, we remember its sounds; hearing the sounds of a brook in the distance, we remember its appearance even though it is hidden from our eyes, and we may associate with it the smell of the woods through which it courses. Associative processes thus unite memory traces with the immediate experience of any one or of several of the various sense organs, enriching and giving meaning and totality to the experience.

Both kinds of associative processes (between perception and movement and among sense organs) may occur simultaneously with the presentation of stimuli, or they may occur after time elapses between the presentation of the stimuli from one organ and those from another, or between the presentation of the stimuli and the response.

The ability to integrate stimuli occurring simultaneously is differentiated from associative transfer, which is the ability to remember

---

* Piaget (1966) uses the term "sensori-motor schemata" to describe the simultaneous perceptual and motor assimilation that characterizes the behavior of an infant. Innate reflex associations are present in the human fetus, and discriminative sensori-motor responses have been demonstrated as early as two weeks after birth (Bower, 1966).

and to integrate percepts and movements occurring in different sense organs separated by time.* Intersensory association and transfer are of particular importance to human beings in their continuing adaptation to their environments.

Associative Processes and Teaching

The associative abilities discussed in this chapter need to be continuously developed and practiced by children and young adults. Even older adults need practice so that they do not lose their ability to react speedily and correctly to the stimuli in their environment.

A good teacher automatically and intuitively trains the associative processes. She knows that maximum efficiency in any task — whether it be driving a car, using a toothbrush, tying knots, mastering swimming strokes, acquiring number facts, or typing by touch — requires that many associative processes become automatic through training and practice.

All learning, and specifically school learning, depends upon the ability to form associations. When the teacher dictates and the children listen and write, an association between auditory perception and movement is required. Association between auditory and visual processes is involved when a child reads a book silently. He must associate the visual stimulus of the printed word with its auditory image. When children sing music from a score, they must associate the visual stimuli with the auditory image and produce the corresponding vocalization. When a child learns that the front of a ship is called "fore" and the back "aft," he forms associations between auditory stimuli, the words that express them, and their meanings.

When any of the associative processes is disturbed, all learning is inhibited. The all-pervasive global disturbances in children with learning difficulties are characterized by difficulties in associative processes. Birch and Belmont (1964, 1965) have shown that even in a normal child the integration of sensory impressions is acquired only gradually. Piaget (1954) has postulated that the ability to integrate the experiences from different senses is learned.

According to Barsch (1967), a child with learning difficulties may be unable to integrate the perceptions that he receives through his

---

*Birch and Belmont (1964, 1965) demonstrated intersensory transfer by first presenting geometric forms visually to children and requiring them later to recognize the same stimuli through touch. They had to choose while blindfolded the forms they had previously seen. Birch also reversed the process and asked the children to try to recognize visually the forms they had first explored through touch.

various sense organs and may live in a world of diversified visual, auditory, olfactory, gustatory, and other sense impressions. Strauss and Lehtinen (1947) and Werner (1957) also have found that it is difficult for the brain-injured child to recognize with one sense organ what he has experienced with another.

The following provides a structured framework to help the teacher consciously plan and select appropriate and effective training methods for her class. Training in associative processes, when translated into classroom practice, involves the entire curriculum and every grade.

Associative Processes and Movement Education

Movement education provides a natural situation for improving associative processes in normal children as well as those with learning difficulties. As explained before, these associative processes fall into three major categories:

1. Associating various perceptions (input) with motor responses (output). Such associations are visual-motor (playing hopscotch); auditory-motor (following directions); and motor-kinesthetic (involved in all movements, but especially those that involve conscious awareness of the movement).

2. Integrating perceptions (input) from more than one sense organ. Climbing requires kinesthetic, tactile, and visual integration; copying a dance movement with musical accompaniment requires visual, auditory, and kinesthetic integration.

3. Associating present stimuli with earlier experiences, thus giving meaning to present stimuli.*

Integration of different perceptions occurs in all movement that is guided by vision because visual stimuli are integrated with kinesthetic stimuli, feedback from the muscles being indispensable for

---

*The teacher can facilitate associations in such a way that learning of new facts becomes almost automatic. Such an approach is used in programmed textbooks and programs for teaching machines. Children, in associating various aspects of the subject matter, can arrive at underlying principles.

The teacher may also let the children themselves try to retrieve and fit together different associations to arrive at a conclusion. This is called the discovery method, and it requires much more active participation from the learner.

Mosston (1966) has used and described a discovery approach in physical education. Dalcroze and Laban built their methods of creative movement on it, but they use less verbalization and rely more directly on the "language of the body." Our own approach combines the development of associations through and of movement, as well as that of associations mediated by language (see Chapter 5).

guiding movement. Movement is thus characterized by the association between input and output, and it nearly always involves the integration of input from at least two senses — the visual and the kinesthetic.

The teacher who is aware of the importance of the close association of all sensory stimuli with movement will ensure that she elicits movement during movement education through visual, auditory, kinesthetic, and tactile stimulation. (See Chapter 11.)

The children should reproduce movements that they see performed by others; they should get directions for movements from the teacher's voice or from a tambourine or other musical instrument; they should perform movement sequences while concentrating on the stimuli coming from within their own bodies; they should have opportunities to develop their tactile sense in an activity such as climbing.

There are no controlled research studies that demonstrate that the development of associative abilities through movement education has direct bearing on the acquisition and enhancement of academic skills. It has not been proved that children who learn to react immediately to commands in movement education or to follow rhythms or to pattern their movements to music will be better able to integrate the visual stimulus of the printed word with the auditory memory of the sound of the word. But clinical observation as well as theoretical considerations indicate that increasing children's movement skills promotes their ability to integrate multiple stimuli. One can safely say that if children become able to integrate the multiple stimuli of their environments and so react to them, their total adaptation will improve. And an improved way of relating to the total environment is almost certain to be reflected in improved classroom performance.

Training Visual-Motor Association, Transfer, and Visual Perception

Vision and movement are so closely interwoven that it is usual to speak of visual-motor tasks and of visual-motor coordination. These are often regarded as the most important aspects of sensory-motor functions and sometimes even as their only educationally relevant aspects. Certain programs that focus on prevention and remediation of learning difficulties have been greatly influenced by an optometric point of view (such as Kephart's, 1960; Barsch's, 1965; and Getman's, 1962). These programs center around both visual-perceptual and motor tasks and pay particular attention to visual-motor coordination. They introduce numerous physical exercises as well as perceptual and visual-motor activities, such as writing or drawing on the chalkboard. Barsch includes the training of other sense organs also while focusing on vision.

These associative abilities do indeed need to be developed optimally; but it needs to be emphasized that movement is not always guided by vision. Blind people often move very skillfully. For the guidance and execution of movements, kinesthetic stimuli are even more important than vision.

This fact in no way diminishes the importance of manipulatory or other activities that develop eye-hand coordination or of the whole-body movements guided by vision. Such activities should be part of all educational curricula, and they are especially necessary for children with learning difficulties. Vision guides the hand in most activities. In games that involve throwing and catching, vision guides the ball or beanbag to its target as well as the hand that catches it. It directs the hands in arts and crafts activities, such as model-making, leather tooling, drawing, and painting. It indicates the height of the jump necessary to clear the obstacle. But vision usually defines the goal, such as *where* the runner should stop or turn or the skier shift weight. It does not guide the *manner* of the movement, as of the legs in running, the body thrust in jumping, or the shift of weight in skiing. It is kinesthesia, rather than vision, that guides each phase of all movement.

It may be of help to clarify the differences between visual-motor association, visual-motor transfer, and visual perception. In visual-motor association, the visual and motor acts occur together. Visual-motor transfer, on the other hand, is what takes place when a visual stimulus — a geometric pattern, for example — has to be reproduced. The response follows the presentation of the stimulus. Visual perception is the ability to recognize and discriminate visual stimuli.

Some children are unable to reproduce a simple pattern, an inability that is often taken to be a visual perceptual difficulty. But many of these children are able to match correctly figures that they cannot draw, proving that it is not their perception that is defective, but rather the ability to reproduce figures (Abercrombie, 1964). The difficulty in these cases is most likely to be one of visual-motor transfer. Training in perception, in visual-motor association, and in transfer are all part of a balanced educational program.

If a child has difficulty in visual-motor transfer, it will readily become apparent in movement education, inasmuch as movement education includes the translation of visual stimuli into movements. When the teacher demonstrates to the children a movement by doing it herself or by showing a picture, the children, to perform the movement, must make visual-motor transfers. If it is evident that a child is unable to make visual-motor transfers, it might be necessary to reinforce the visual models by giving verbal directions and requiring the child to repeat the directions before carrying them out. The importance of verbalization is discussed in Chapter 9. If pictures are used to elicit a movement, they should at first show only simple body positions and gradually become more complex.

Training Auditory-Motor Association and Transfer

Except for blind people, movement in everyday living is guided much less by auditory perceptions than by visual ones, although auditory perceptions do play a role. We pull to the curb when the car motor sounds different from usual or when we hear a siren.

As with visual-motor association and visual-motor transfer, we can distinguish between auditory-motor association and auditory-motor transfer. Auditory-motor association refers to simultaneous hearing and doing. Dancing to music is an excellent example of this kind of association. Auditory-motor transfer refers to a process in which the auditory stimulus is followed by the motor act. Auditory-motor transfer occurs, for example, when the teacher gives verbal directions to the children, and the children follow the directions. Difficulty in following directions and its treatment in the framework of movement education has been discussed in Chapter 6 in the section on receptive language. (A child may be unable to follow directions because of receptive language difficulties but may also be unable to follow directions because of associative difficulties.)

In every class there seems to be at least one child, and usually more, who cannot follow directions correctly or who seems to be excessively slow in carrying them out. The teacher may say to the class, "Take your books and open them to page 7." She observes that while most of the children follow the directions easily and speedily, Johnny seems unable to accomplish the task even though he can repeat the directions without hesitation. Further observation may show that Johnny's difficulties occur when he has to initiate the task described in verbal directions, although at other times he is usually quite skillful.

Such children as Johnny often improve greatly as they become used to following instructions during the movement education period, particularly if the teacher makes sure before giving instructions that the children are paying full attention. She should begin with simple commands and later give sequences of directions. The teacher may say, for example, "Now listen closely and try to remember all that I say. I'm going to name several movements that you will try to do one after the other without adding any or leaving any out. We call this a movement sequence. Are you listening? Good! Now . . . " Then she proceeds with the directions.

Training Motor-Kinesthetic Association

Kinesthetic stimuli are the sensations that originate in the muscles during movement. Kinesthetic feedback is indispensable for directed movement; it is impossible to perform any conscious directed movement without such feedback, although kinesthetic feedback is largely registered unconsciously. We are usually much less aware of its role in guiding movement than we are of the role of vision.

Certain neurological damage results in a disturbance of kinesthetic feedback. When this disturbance is severe, a person may be unable to produce any voluntary movement. If the disturbance is less severe, the person may have difficulty in touching any part of his body that he cannot see, and if he closes his eyes, he may not be able to balance or to move without falling. These tasks are given as tests in neurological examinations because they reveal whether a person has defective kinesthesia.

Making children more aware of muscle feedback, hence of the movements of their bodies, is an important goal of movement education. They will gain in coordination, skill and grace of movement, and be more successful in sports and games. Improvement of body awareness is an important educational goal for slow learners, since they are often clumsy and poorly coordinated.

Training Tactile-Motor Association

Tactile stimuli are also important for some movements, such as tracing. They are closely integrated with kinesthetic stimuli in the perception of surfaces. Children should learn to direct their movements by tactile stimuli through an activity such as climbing a ladder, which involves close contact with a surface.

Training Association Between Incoming and Stored Experiences

Association between stimuli currently present in the environment and the previous experiences of a child is the very essence of giving meaning to the present experience. As discussed in the footnote on page 102, associations may be formed either inductively or deductively. The teacher of movement education must be concerned not only with relating certain exercises and commands to those given to the children in the past, but she must also be concerned with encouraging the children to discover certain principles for themselves. An example of the first is "Yesterday you sat on discs placed on the floor in a circle. Today sit the same way. Pretend the discs are still there." An example of the second is "What happens when you kick the football near its top? On its middle? Near the bottom? Why? How would you kick it for a field goal?"

Mosston (1966) gives carefully delineated steps for guiding the learner from awareness of a problem to discovery of its solution within the context of physical education. The reader is referred to Mosston's book and to Chapter 5 of this book.

As discussed in this chapter, movement education can train the following associative abilities:

Skill	Examples
Visual-motor association	Catching a ball Throwing a basketball through a hoop Tossing horsehoes Running hurdles Guiding an object, such as a hockey puck or a basketball, over a path
Visual-motor transfer	Reproducing a movement Reproducing a position shown in a picture. Reading directions for an exercise and following them Executing a football play after chalkboard demonstration
Auditory-motor association	Dancing to music Doing the movements of a barn dance as instructed by the caller Interpreting signals of pitch or tone in creative movement (e.g., low, deep sound leads to heavy steps with body low to ground)
Auditory-motor transfer	Listening to a series of instructions for a movement sequence and then carrying them out Interpreting with movements a story or poem that has been read Reproducing a rhythmic sequence (by clapping, tapping, or with a tambourine)
Motor-kinesthetic association	Body awareness exercises Balance exercises

Maintaining position on a balance board
Shifting weight in skiing

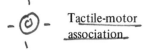

Tactile-motor
association

Climbing (jungle gym, tree, etc.)
Crawling through a tunnel
Tracing a maze blindfolded
Tracing sandpaper letter patterns blindfolded
Maintaining footing in muddy water

Works Cited

Abercrombie, M. L. J., Gardiner, P. A., Hansen, E., Jonckherre, J., Lindson, R. L., Solomon, G., and Tyson, M. C. Visual perceptual and visuomotor impairment in physically handicapped children. *Perceptual and Motor Skills,* 1964, **18**, 561-625. (Monogr. Suppl. 3-V18.)

Barsch, R. H. *Achieving Perceptual-Motor Efficiency.* Vol. 1 (Perceptual-Motor Curriculum Series). Seattle: Special Child Publications, 1967.

Barsch, R. H. *A Movigenic Curriculum.* Bulletin No. 25, Bureau of Handicapped Children. Madison, Wis.: State Department of Public Instruction, 1965.

Birch, H. G., and Belmont, L. Auditory-visual integration, intelligence and reading ability in school children. *Perceptual and Motor Skills,* 1965, **20**, 295-305.

Birch, H. G., and Belmont, L. Auditory-visual integration in normal and retarded readers. *American Journal of Orthopsychiatry,* 1964, **34**, 825-861.

Bruner, J. S. *Toward a Theory of Instruction.* Cambridge, Mass.: Harvard Univ. Press, 1966.

Bower, T. G. R. The visual world of infants. *Scientific American,* 1966, **215**, 80-92.

English, H. B., and English, A. C. *A Comprehensive Dictionary of Psychological and Psychoanalytical Terms.* New York: McKay, 1958.

Getman, G. N. *How to Develop Your Child's Intelligence.* Luverne, Minn.: Author, 1962.

Hebb, D. O. Concerning imagery. *Psychological Review,* 1968, **75**, 466-477.

Hebb, D. O. A neuropsychological theory. In S. Koch (Ed.), *Psychology: A Study of a Science.* New York: McGraw-Hill, 1959, 622-643.

Kephart, N. C. *The Slow Learner in the Classroom.* Columbus, Ohio: Charles E. Merrill, 1960.

Krech, D., Rosenzweig, M. R., and Bennett, E. L. Relations between brain chemistry and problem solving among cats raised in enriched and impoverished environments. *Journal of Comparative and Physiological Psychology,* 1962, **55**, 801-807.

Mosston, M. *Teaching Physical Education.* Columbus, Ohio: Charles E. Merrill, 1966.

Piaget, J. *The Construction of Reality in the Child.* New York: Basic Books, 1954.

Piaget, J. *The Psychology of Intelligence.* Totona, N.J.: Littlefield, Adams, 1966. (First published in French, 1947.)

Piaget, J. *Six Psychological Studies.* New York: Random House, 1967.

Strauss, A. A., and Lehtinen, L. E. *Psychopathology and Education of the Brain-Injured Child.* Vol. 1. New York: Grune & Stratton, 1947.

Werner, H. *Comparative Psychology of Mental Development.* (Rev. ed.) New York: International Universities Press, 1957. (First published 1940.)

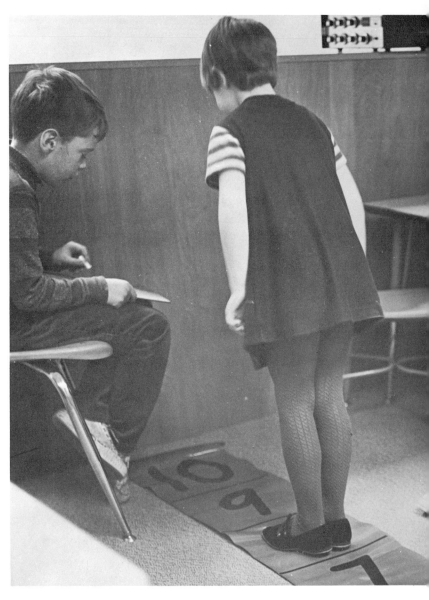

This little girl using the number line learns that 8 + 2 = 10. The boy writes it down.

Academics and Movement Education

Movement education can beneficially affect academic learning, directly and indirectly.

Directly, games and techniques employing whole-body movements can be used to teach mathematics, reading, and other academic subjects. Physical movement is particularly helpful for teaching academic skills that involve perception of spatial relationships. It therefore provides many techniques for teaching mathematics.

Indirectly, motor efficiency affects the total ability to learn by influencing the self-image (see Chapter 4) and by promoting basic abilities, such as memory, perceptual skills, concentration, orientation in time and space, associative processes, and the ability to solve problems — abilities that underlie the learning process and enable children to learn both in and out of school (see Chapters 6 and 9).* A further effect upon the capacity to learn is the relief from tension afforded by the opportunity for free movement after long hours of sitting. The provision of frequent short periods of motor activity is especially beneficial for children who are under strain in the classroom because they are disturbed, are anxious, or are slow learners. If there are occasional breaks in which they perform relaxing exercises, they are able to concentrate better on their academic work later on. Or if they practice charades or perform other mimetic games, they gain in their ability to express themselves in gestures and movement, and they also tend to return to their work more relaxed and with increased energy and confidence.

Motor Proficiency and Academic Learning

Barsch (1967) and others have suggested that the early development of perceptual-motor abilities is conducive to proficiency in school

---

*Action accompanied by appropriate verbalization makes a difference in learning. Sonstroem (1966) reported that first-grade children allowed to perform the necessary manipulation of materials and required to describe verbally what they were doing and what happened as a result of their actions were highly successful in inducing recognition of the conservation of solids (recognizing that mass remains identical despite transformation of shape).

learning, especially reading. Kephart regards perceptual-motor training as a necessary preliminary to reading instruction for children
with learning difficulties, and it is recommended that such training
precede, accompany, and be integrated with reading instruction. He
(see Godfrey and Kephart, 1969) believes that children with inflexible movement patterns cannot learn efficiently until this disability
has been amended, because, in his view, reading skills, especially
those influenced by visual perception, depend on a certain degree
of response flexibility and control. Kephart differentiates, however,
between movement skills as such and what he calls "response generalizations."

An over-simplified and over-generalized assumption that improvement in movement efficiency will always lead to better academic
achievement is erroneous, however. It is based on the belief that
because psychological abilities normally develop in a certain sequence,
remediation procedures must recapitulate this sequence. It is assumed that training in any psychological ability should be undertaken only after attainment of a certain degree of proficiency in
the abilities that developmentally precede it. A degree of proficiency
in sensory-motor skills, for instance, is assumed before training in
perceptual skills is undertaken.

The positive correlations found between health, vigor, the degree
of physical ability, and scholastic achievement are also cited in support of the belief that training in movement skills will necessarily
result in higher school achievement.

It needs to be emphasized, however, that there is no proof that
children with movement deficiencies cannot learn academic skills
and subject matter. In fact, clinical experience brings proof to the
contrary. Even children with gross deficiencies in movement, such
as those with cerebral palsy,* as well as those with lesser handicaps —
the "clumsy" children — are often proficient in academic learning
and intellectual pursuits. We agree with Cratty (1969) that movement deficiencies may contribute to learning difficulties, that both
may result from the same underlying cause, and that the presence
of movement difficulties does not usually affect a child's learning
difficulties directly.

Careful research with infants (Gibson, 1960; Fantz, 1966; Bower,
1966), with animals (John, 1968), and with adults has shown that

---

*Abercrombie (1966) has shown that children in late childhood and early
teens who have lacked movement skills from birth because of cerebral palsy
may perform on an equal level of intelligence and perception with normal
children. The degree of the physical handicap did not permit prediction of
the future level of intelligence.

observation of movement rather than movement itself is crucial for the development of perceptual and conceptual abilities. Human beings can react to stimuli either by perceiving or by moving. Perceiving can occur with no other movements than those of the eyeballs (visual exploration) and of the lenses (focusing).

Observation of movement sequences is an important aspect of movement education because of its implications for academic learning. Rohwer (1968) and his associates have demonstrated in a series of experiments that watching an action sequence, particularly when combined with a description of the sequence, is a powerful facilitator of certain forms of rote learning in young children. Bower (1967) has shown that instructions to imagine an action enabled adults to remember pairs of words (both immediately and after a delay) more often than if no imagined action was involved in the instructions. Rote learning is highly correlated with school achievement, as indicated by research and observation (Stevenson et al., 1968). It would therefore appear that movement and action, preferably accompanied by verbalization, can improve children's academic performance.

These considerations do not contradict the importance of movement education. Rather, they indicate the importance of providing experiences and opportunities for observation and perception *in addition* to teaching movement skills. (See Chapter 11.) The teacher needs to be aware that children are involved in important learning activities when they simply observe the movement of others.

Another important conclusion is that academic learning should not be postponed because of motor deficiency. Training in both areas must be undertaken simultaneously.

Methods for Teaching Academic Skills

During the period specifically set aside for movement education, training in movement skills must be the main goal, and academic teaching can only be integrated to a degree. But during the rest of the school day physical activities can be freely used to promote and reinforce the learning of subject matter and skills.

Arithmetic

Games employing whole-body movements can help teach all four arithmetic processes, including fractions and basic mathematical laws. Learning arithmetic through games is not a modern fad. Montessori understood that children can be helped immeasurably to learn number concepts through the use of play, dance, and specific body movements. The egg crating games described below were observed first-hand in a Montessori school in Vienna 40 years ago.

Methods using movement skills teach number concepts better than any other single method because visual stimuli, auditory stimuli, and movement reinforce each other, and concepts of distance, comparison, and sets are dramatically illustrated. The teacher must understand, however, that for optimum results in teaching mathematics the movement skills approach must be combined with many others. It does not replace other teaching methods — it supplements them.

During the movement education period itself, the children can learn to use numbers for denoting size, distance, and quantity without jeopardizing the main objectives of the session. Many activities, such as taking turns, repeating an exercise a certain number of times, and keeping score, provide opportunities for counting and for the use of cardinal and ordinal numbers.

An important task in learning basic mathematical concepts is matching numbers — learning the equivalence of numbers. If, for example, there are four children and each is given a hoop, the children learn that four hoops are needed. They learn that a number is an abstraction that can pertain to anything measurable — to units of time and space (minutes, inches), and to quantities (hoops, balls, children, jumps, steps).

Having a child write down the problem and the answer in number line games is important.

Children can also learn to compare sizes and distances during movement education periods, as when they are told: "Take the *longer* rope." "We need *more* children for playing Looby Loo." "Let's run to the gate — it's *farther* than the tree." This informal method of teaching mathematical relationships may become more formal as time progresses.

The teacher may also help the children to form an association between the names of numbers and written numerals by holding up a card with the appropriate numeral written on it every time she says a number. If, for example, she says, "Five children go to the swings," she holds up the card with the numeral 5 on it.

The teacher should use visual aids for all arithmetic games. Even on the playground she should have a chalkboard, a magnetic board, a slate, or a feltboard on which she can exhibit number facts that the children are acting out or on which a child can write the numerical fact that the other children are illustrating by movement. Each child should also write on the board or slate a numerical problem, such as $3 + 2 =$, while another child acts it out. Then the first child should fill in the answer. This will help the children to understand the process of addition more fully. It will also help them to learn to work in pairs.

Games that integrate arithmetic with movement education follow. Their primary purpose is to teach mathematical concepts. They are given in the order of their difficulty, and they may be used in nursery school, kindergarten, or first grade — wherever work with numbers is introduced. In the higher grades, they may be followed by activities extending the children's number concepts.

Number Line Games — Arithmetic Hopscotch

The number line is made up of ten 24-inch squares painted on the surface of the playground and numbered from "Start" (or 0) through 10. It is used for Arithmetic Hopscotch games. Since children should not have to wait in line for any length of time but should be active, it is best to use more than one number line if there are more than eight to ten children in a group.

Game 1: Hop a Number

This game helps children grasp the equivalence of numbers and also makes them aware of the sequence of numbers (seriation).

A child is told by the teacher to hop to a certain numbered square on the number line. The child, who begins at the "Start" square, then finds out that to land on the square marked with a certain numeral he must make an equal number of hops — four hops to reach the square marked 4, five to reach the square marked 5, and so on.

Game 2: Find Your Number

This game, like the preceding one, helps children become aware of the sequence of numbers.

The teacher first covers the numerals on the number line with cards big enough to cover the numeral on each square. She then gives each child a card bearing a numeral corresponding to one on the number line. Each child in turn runs to the square that he thinks corresponds to his number and removes the cover card to see if the numerals match.

The teacher should continue the game, giving the children different numerals each time, until they are thoroughly acquainted with the position of each number.

Game 3: Find Your Neighbor

In this game, the children learn to find the next number. They also become acquainted with partial counting and the concept of adding one.

The teacher tells the children that the square next to a given square is called its "neighbor." Each child in turn is then "given" a number. One child, for example, is given the number 3. He runs to the square numbered 3, and then he makes a single jump and "finds his neighbor," number 4. As he jumps he shouts "3 and 1 are 4," looking at the numbers as he does so. If a child has no difficulty in verbalizing number facts, such as "3 and 1 are 4" or "6 and 1 are 7," he may practice variations in jumping, such as landing on one foot or clapping while jumping, in order to avoid boredom and further his movement skills.

Game 4: Find the One Before You

This game introduces children to the concept of subtracting one, and it teaches them to count backward.

The teacher points out that each number has two neighbors, one of which is before it and one after it. Each child is asked to stand on a square and then jump backward, saying first the number from which he starts and then the number on which he lands — for example, "4, 3."

The teacher should explain the meanings of the words plus and minus. Games 3 and 4 can then be played again with the children saying "plus one" as they jump forward and "minus one" as they jump backward. This step prepares children for addition and subtraction with numbers other than 1.

Game 5: Red and Green

This game introduces children to number facts.

The teacher gives each child a green card and a red card, each of which is marked with a different numeral. He is told to look first at the numeral on the green card and to run to the square on the number line with the same numeral. When he has reached the square, he looks at the numeral on the red card and jumps forward the correct number of squares. For example, if he has a green 3 and a red 2, he runs to 3 and then jumps two more squares, landing on 5. As he does so, he shouts "3 plus 2 equal 5!" At first the number of jumps (red card) should be restricted to one or two.

This game may also be played by having a child jump backward. For instance, his green card may have the numeral 5 on it, and his red card 2. He runs to square 5 and jumps backward two squares, landing on square 3 and calling out "5 minus 2 equal 3!"

The children may avoid errors by saying aloud the appropriate numbers on the number lines as they proceed. The integration of verbalization, movement, and visual and auditory stimuli makes the acquisition of number facts easier for most children.

Game 6: Turn Around

Attainment of mathematical concepts and learning of addition and subtraction facts are facilitated if children understand that each arithmetic problem can be reversed; for example, that if $3 + 2 = 5$, $5 - 2$ must $= 3$. This can be taught with the help of physical activity.

The teacher should write number facts on the slate or board and the children should each demonstrate at least one fact and its reverse form by walking or hopping along the number line. For example, the teacher may write $4 + 2 = 6$. A child hops four squares and jumps two more; then the child reverses the problem by hopping back two squares while the teacher writes $6 - 4 = 2$. The child should also discover in this way that $6 - 2 = 4$.

Game 7: Get a Train Ticket

The children should by this time be ready to solve problems involving the missing addend, such as $4 + \ \ = 6$. Playing the train game makes abstract problems more concrete and helps children to understand and solve them. This game introduces children to the concept of the missing addend and place holder without the necessity of using the terms. The mathematical vocabulary depends upon the curriculum and textbooks used in the school. The game is self-correcting.

The teacher says, "Each square is a stop on our train track." Then she poses a problem with a missing addend, such as $2 + \ \ = 5$. "That means, how far is it from the second stop to the fifth stop?" Now one child stands in square 2 on the number line, and, to make it easier to remember that it is the second stop, he is told that this square represents his hometown, which may be called Two Rivers. He is then told to "take a train" to Five Towns (square 5, the fifth stop) by hopping. He must calculate as he does so how many stops the train makes and therefore how much he must pay for his ticket on the basis of one dollar for each stop. The teacher writes the problem on the board: second stop to fifth stop, 2 +   = 5. The child hops from square 2 to square 5, counting the number of hops, or "stops." He then pretends to pay the three-dollar fare. Either the teacher or a child should write the answer in the correct space on the board.

By jumping back, each child may return to his hometown, the number from which he started. He finds that his ticket costs the same in each direction, and that if 2 + 3 = 5, 5 - 3 = 2.

The children should find out at this point that two addition facts can be put in reverse order without changing the sums, such as 2 + 3 = 3 + 2 (commutative law of addition).

These games should be repeated often. The children should be encouraged to make up their own names for the towns, indicating the order of stops with such names as One Oak, Two Rivers, Three Churches, Four Roads, Five Valleys, Six Mountains, Seven Hills, Eight Lakes, Nine Palms, and Ten Pines.

Game 8: Making Several Stops
Using the number line, the children should next learn that a number can be composed of other numbers, thus becoming acquainted with the fact that different addends can combine to make the same sum (a set can be composed of different subsets). For example, 4 + 1 + 1, 1 + 3 + 2, and 1 + 5 all equal 6.

The children should also become aware that numbers can be added in different order. For instance, a child may jump three times, then once, and then twice. The equation is written 3 + 1 + 2 = 6. He is then told to jump 1 + 2 + 3 and write the equation; then to jump 2 + 1 + 3; then 3 + 2 + 1; then 1 + 3 + 2; then 2 + 3 + 1. It is essential that the child's jumps be recorded each time, and that he has an opportunity to review the various orders in which the numbers may be added to equal the same sum.

Game 9: The Railroad Schedule (Finding what addends combine to make a sum)
The children again use the number line. They find out that if a child starts at square 4 and makes one hop, he lands on square 5. If he

starts at square 2, makes one hop, and then two more hops, he also
lands on square 5. The children should be told to take a "slow train"
to find out all of the possible combinations of numbers that will
get them from one station to another. For example, if they are to
go from Two Rivers to Eight Lakes, they can go with any number
of combinations of stops between, such as 2 + 4 + 2; or 2 + 3 + 3.
The teacher is reminded that all examples that are acted out should
also be written with numerals on a slate.

The concept of zero should be introduced next, and "Start" on
the number line should be replaced by 0.

The number line and jumping and hopping games should not be
used so often that the children become bored. To avoid tedium and
provide exercise, the jumping and hopping should be varied. Some
vigorous movement should relieve the mental activity. The children
might, for example, jump as high as possible; turn in the air while
jumping; or jump and land in a crouch position.

The number line may also be used for other games, such as throwing beanbags into given squares or picking up small objects from the
squares.

Egg Crating Games

Nearly all number concepts can be acted out. The teacher will have
many ideas of her own. The following games are examples for advanced children. They teach the concept of dozen and the equaliza-
tion of sets by dividing a set into subsets in various ways. Games
similar to this should be played frequently because they can be used
to help the development of concepts of division, multiplication,
fractions, addition, subtraction, and ordinal and cardinal numbers.
The games may be varied to maintain interest, the children pretend-
ing that they are trees in a forest or sheep in a pen, as well as eggs
in a crate.

For the egg crating games, the teacher should draw twelve squares

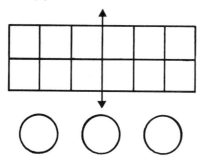

on the floor or playground to indicate an egg carton (page 119). She should also draw three circles outside the squares.

One child stands in each square of the egg carton. Each child in a square has a white paper oval tied around his neck like an apron to show that he is an egg. The teacher tells the eggs to leave the carton, six (one row) marching to the right, the other six to the left. The teacher might say, "Now we have a half-dozen eggs here and a half-dozen eggs there. I see twelve eggs. Twelve eggs are a dozen; six eggs are a half-dozen. Six plus six is twelve. Two sets of six make twelve. Get into your carton again and let's see if we are right. Yes, six plus six is twelve." The children should repeat the movements. One child should be asked to write the problem on the board: 2/12 = 6 and say, "Twelve divided by two is six."

The teacher may then proceed with other problems, such as the following: "Now let's divide our twelve eggs among four families. We will pretend that each family lives in one corner of the room (or playground). If each family gets the same number of eggs, how many will each have? Let's try it out." The teacher asks one child to go to one corner, another to a second corner, and so on until the twelve children are equally divided among the four corners — all of the eggs are divided equally among four families. "Look! There are three eggs for each family; twelve divided by four is three. Let's write it on the board: 4/12 = 3. Now each group of three children march back into the carton. Look, four groups of three is twelve. Let's write that on the board too: 4 x 3 = 12."

In the following type of problem, the three circles near the egg carton are used. One after another, the children in the egg carton run to a circle, a child to each circle in turn. Since four children finally are in each circle, it is discovered that twelve divided by three is four. When the children run back to the carton they see that three sets of four make twelve. By playing the game repeatedly and dividing the dozen eggs in various ways, the children learn the concepts of sets, of division and multiplication, of dozen, and of fractions.

The various aspects of the game should be introduced slowly and the concepts to be learned repeated. Notation is learned and practiced as each new concept is introduced. Each concept should also be practiced in other situations, such as during arithmetic or social science periods.

The games that have been described do not constitute a complete mathematics program. The teacher may add games that she can use in conjunction with the methods she usually uses for the teaching of mathematics in the classroom.

Reading

Games and exercises can involve following written directions, learning letter forms, spelling, listening for vowels and syllables, learning the alphabet, and other reading skills.

Following Written Directions

When children are taught to follow printed or written directions for their movement education exercises, the primary focus is on training the attributes of movement, although reading skills are practiced and associated with movement skills.

Children just beginning to read gain from seeing printed words denoting actions that they carry out. The teacher should first show cards on each of which is printed a verb or preposition, such as *go, stop, skip, hop, walk, turn, up, down.* As she shows each card for the first time, she pronounces the word, and the children carry out the action. But as soon as possible, the children should learn to read the directions and carry out the actions without help from the teacher.

Later she should show a sequence of cards and have the children combine the different movements as smoothly as possible. For example, the teacher may show (1) the card for *go,* and the children walk about; (2) the card for *turn,* and the children turn; (3) the card for *under,* and the children go under a rope or crawl under a table; (4) the card for *out,* and the children take beanbags out of a basket; (5) the card for *throw,* and the children throw the beanbags into the air and catch them; (6) the card for *into,* and the children put the beanbags back into the basket.

When the children can read single words and correctly carry out the actions, the teacher should show short sentence cards for the children to read and respond to, such as *Run to me. Get the ball.*

More advanced readers should be shown longer sentences and eventually sequences of sentences. For example, the teacher may write: (1) *Walk across the playground like a crab,* or (2) *Run toward the slide and jump over the balance board.*

When the children are proficient in following written directions, the teacher can divide the class into several groups, each group working together to solve the movement problem given in written directions. The teacher should prepare several sets of instructions in advance to avoid writing during the movement education period. All directions for a group should be written on a single roll of paper, and the rolls should be fastened to the gymnasium walls where each group can look at its own. The children may need considerable time to work out each sequence, and the teacher should give help when needed.

Examples for children reading at about high third-grade (or fourth-grade) level follow:

Group 1:

1. Get the long jump rope.

2. Two of you turn the rope while the others line up away from the rope. Try to keep the rope turning.

3. The first child in line runs to the rope and jumps it ten times. Run to the back of the line when you have jumped. The next child takes a turn.

4. The last two children to jump take the places of the two children turning the rope, who get the next turns to jump.

5. Could you all jump without being touched by the rope? All of you who were hit by the rope, try it this way. Stand next to the rope before it is turned. Then jump when it is swinging. This is an easier way to start.

Group 2:

1. Skip across the room three times. Each choose your own path.

2. Gallop across the room three times. Each choose your own path.

3. Now change from walking to skipping while crossing the room three times. Line up behind Lisa. She is the leader.

4. Next gallop and then change to walking. Line up behind John. John is the leader.

5. Last, each try your own way of changing from galloping to skipping and then to walking. Don't bump into each other.

6. When you have finished, come to me.

Group 3:

1. Each of you take a beanbag and a bowling pin.

2. Put the bowling pin on the floor and walk backward five steps.

3. Face the pin, holding the beanbag.

4. Try to throw your beanbag so that it hits the pin.

5. Get the beanbag and throw it again.

6. Whenever you throw correctly three times in a row, take a step backward and throw from there.

7. Find the longest distance from which you can throw the beanbag correctly three times in a row.

8. Measure the distance with the tape measure.

9. Dan should be scorekeeper and write down the distance each of you throws.

When the groups have completed their assignments, the teacher should ask two groups to sit down while the other group shows and discusses what it has done. The children may ask questions and discuss difficulties. Then the groups should be rotated.

In another activity, the teacher may label apparatus and areas of the playground or gymnasium. She then gives the children directions that oblige them to read the labels and go over an obstacle course according to the directions.

She might, for instance, label the jungle gym *Big Mountain;* a ladder, *Tall Tower;* a wooden obstacle, *Steep Rock;* lines drawn on the ground or floor, *Wide Ditch;* space for running, *Large Meadow;* the balance beam, *Narrow Bridge;* a log, *Round Log;* and a circle on the floor, *Fish Pond.* She then holds up cards on which have been printed directions similar to the following:

Climb over Big Mountain.	Climb Steep Rock.
Jump over Wide Ditch.	Run across Large Meadow.
Climb Tall Tower.	Cross over Narrow Bridge.
Run around Fish Pond.	Slide over Round Log.

Letter Forms and Spelling

In the following games, the focus is on learning a reading skill; not on movement skills. Movement is used only as a teaching method.

Playground markings can be helpful in teaching the forms of the letters of the alphabet. If a figure is sufficiently complex, it can contain almost all letter forms. *

16'

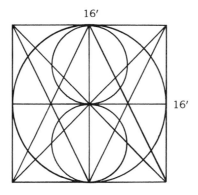

16'

*This pattern was suggested by Bryant Cratty, oral communication.

Other playground markings can aid letter recognition and spelling. In learning the spatial location of letters, children can also be helped to learn the sequence of the letters and thus alphabetizing.

The teacher should print the alphabet in painted markings of 24-inch squares in the following way:

A	B	C	D	E	F	G
H	I	J	K	L	M	N
O	P	Q	R	S	T	U
V	W	X	Y	Z		

One child should be asked to spell MOTHER, for example, by first walking to the M square, clapping, and saying the letter; then walking in turn to the squares containing the other letters in the word, clapping, and saying the letter in each. After spelling a word, each child should write the word on a small slate. If a child does not write a word down immediately he may learn left-to-right reversals. For example, in spelling the word *fed* on the playground, the child walks from right to left, not left to right. If the word is written, the child will be helped to remember the correct order of the letters.

Letters can also be printed out of sequence in such a way that each row and column contains a number of consonants and at least one vowel. The children should be asked to see how many words they can spell in each row and column, walking or running between the letters. Again, each word should be written.

B	A	D	N	K	C
J	O	T	L	X	Y
H	W	I	P	Z	A
U	Q	E	T	S	O
R	A	F	M	S	T
Y	G	R	A	V	B

Vowels and Syllables

The teacher should say words and ask the children to take a short step when they hear a short vowel in a word and to take a giant step when they hear a long vowel. Or they may then be asked to jump (once, twice, three times) to indicate the number of syllables in a word.

Body Alphabet

Recently, Barsch (1965) and Kirschner (1965) have advocated the use of the whole body as an aid to learning the sounds and names of letters.

We have prepared at the Center alphabet cards that emphasize body movements.* For example, a child may imitate the form of the letter *k* by standing erect, one foot forward and one hand up as if holding a scepter, a regal posture that connotes *k* for *king.* For other letters, other methods are used that involve movement, either perceived or performed. For instance, a child may carry an imaginary pack on his back to experience the shape of the letter *p.* He walks across the room with sagging shoulders, bent forward as if carrying a heavy pack on his back, saying "*P*at carries a heavy *p*ack. How heavy *P*at's *p*ack is." These methods are used instead of the body alphabet used by Barsch or Kirschner because the human body does not conform to the shape of all letters, and we want to avoid having two children together form a single letter. If they do, each child gains a kinesthetic experience of only part of the whole letter.

Barsch also uses other techniques for learning letters, such as walking or running along the outline of a letter drawn on the floor. After a child has done that, he "traces" the letter by walking or running the shape of it without benefit of an outline on the floor. This exercise requires a child to translate from two dimensions (the letter as shown) to three dimensions (body movement). It also helps him to form a mental picture of the letter.†

---

*For an experimental set of illustrations and a discussion of them, the reader is referred to the Frostig Alphabet Cards, available from the authors.

†It is usually much more difficult for a child to run a perceived pattern on the floor than to draw it on the chalkboard or on paper (Keogh, 1968).

We have also found clinically that it is very difficult for children with visual perceptual disturbances to translate from two dimensions into three dimensions. The exercise, therefore, is of value not only for reading but for orientation in space and for visual perceptual development.

Works Cited

Abercrombie, M. L. J. Body image and draw-a-man test in cerebral palsy. *Developmental Medicine and Child Neurology*, 1966, **8**, 9-15.

Barsch, R. H. *Achieving Perceptual-Motor Efficiency.* Vol. 1 (Perceptual-Motor Curriculum Series). Seattle: Special Child Publications, 1967.

Barsch, R. H. *A Movigenic Curriculum.* Bulletin No. 25, Bureau of Handicapped Children. Madison, Wis.: State Department of Public Instruction, 1965.

Bower, G. H. Mental imagery and memory. Mimeographed paper, Department of Psychology, Stanford University, Palo Alto, Calif., 1967.

Bower, T. G. R. The visual world of infants. *Scientific American,* 1966, **215**, 80-92.

Cratty, B. J. Rationale for and principles of perceptual-motor training. In G. Schiffman and D. Carter (Eds.), *Multidisciplinary Approaches to Learning Disorders.* Chicago: John Wiley, 1969.

Fantz, R. Pattern discrimination and selective attention as determinants of perceptual development from birth. In A. H. Kidd and J. L. Rivoire (Eds.), *Perceptual Development in Children.* New York: International Universities Press, 1966.

Gibson, E., and Walk, R. D. The visual cliff. *Scientific American,* 1960, **202**, 64-71.

Godfrey, B. B., and Kephart, N. C. *Movement Patterns and Motor Education.* New York: Appleton-Century-Crofts, 1969.

John, R. Observation learning in cats. *Science,* 1968, **159** (3822), 1489-1491.

Keogh, B., and Keogh, J. Pattern walking: A dimension of visuomotor performance. *Exceptional Children*, 1968, **34** (8), 617-618.

Kirschner, A. J. Body alphabet. Paper presented at the meeting of the New York Allstate Congress of Optometry, October, 1965.

Rohwer, W. D., Jr. Mental mnemonics in early learning. *Teacher's College Record,* 1968, **70**, 213-226.

Sonstroem, A. On the conservation of solids. In J. S. Bruner, R. R. Oliver, P. M. Greenfield, et al. (Eds.), *Studies in Cognitive Growth.* New York: John Wiley, 1966, 208-224.

Stevenson, H. W., Hale, G. A., Klein, R. E., and Miller, L. K. Interrelations and correlates in children's learning and problem solving. *Monographs of the Society for Research in Child Development,* 1968, **33** (7, Serial No. 123).

Chapter 9

Movement Education for Children with Learning Difficulties

Children with learning difficulties are found in all classrooms, not only in special classes. This is especially true in school districts in which the socioeconomic level is low. This chapter is, therefore, of great concern to *all* teachers. Teachers are strongly urged not to disregard this chapter on the basis that they are not concerned with classes specifically designated for children with learning difficulties.

Some educators believe that programs for children with learning difficulties should be based primarily on physical education combined with perceptual training. Drowatsky (1965), for example, states that skills such as running, jumping, and throwing should form the basic elements of such a program.

Kephart (1960), Barsch (1965), and others have developed physical education programs especially designed for neurologically handicapped children, retarded children, and slow learners. Influenced partly by neurological considerations, partly by an optometric viewpoint, these educators are interested mainly in the relationship between visual perception and movement. Their programs involve training in laterality, sensory-motor functions, visual perception, and body reaction to gravity. Although an underpinning of coherent scientific theory is not yet available, and the claims concerning the results of these remedial programs are not clearly buttressed by experimental data, they provide excellent suggestions and should be carefully studied by all teachers of children with special educational needs.

The psychomotor education program developed by Naville and Ajuriaguerra (1967) is based on neurophysiological and developmental foundations and on Dalcroze's suggestions for "rhythmics," or, as we would say now, a form of movement education. Psychomotor education is designed as part of the total educational program for a child. It embodies an excellent approach for working with neurologically handicapped children, particularly in its stress on inner controls (self-control). Its theoretical framework and philosophy of education is very similar to our own. We hope that detailed descriptions of this program will soon be available in English.

We believe that all children need a varied movement education program based on the attributes of movement (Chapter 12). This program therefore also includes exercises for body awareness (Chapter 4), creative movement (Chapters 5 and 11), integration of training in movement education with training in psychological functions (Chapter 6), and integration of movement education with academics (Chapter 8). Chapters 4 and 6 are of special importance for children with learning difficulties and should therefore be studied carefully by teachers working with such groups.

The entire program is applicable to all children, including those with handicaps, if adaptations are made that take into account the varied needs of these children. The adaptations are the focus of this chapter. In addition, other subjects are discussed that have relevance for children with learning difficulties. Such children are found in all classrooms. As the teacher needs to take into account the needs of every child in the class, this chapter should be read by all classroom teachers.

Characteristics of Children with Learning Difficulties

A great variety of terms have been used in referring to children with learning difficulties — terms that point to different conceptualizations, to different etiology, and to different symptoms. The perceptually disturbed child, the brain injured child, the so-called Strauss syndrome child,[*] the neuropsychologically disturbed child, the interjacent child,[†] the learning handicapped child are all examples of these terms.[††]

Not only do the terms vary, but descriptions of the behavior of children designated by the same term also vary. Some authorities describe mainly children with perceptual or perceptual-motor disturbances, some hyperactive children, others slow learners, and still

---

[*]Characterized by restlessness, disorganization, impulsivity, and inability to concentrate, attributed to a neurological defect.

[†]Doll (1965) defined the interjacent child ". . . as one who is in-between, marginal or weak but not altogether deficient in his aptitudes and the use of these aptitudes for successful learning . . . . These hazy defects and deficiencies are apparent in various modalities, sensory, neuromuscular, intellectual, social and other. . . ."

[††]See also Clements, S. D., Minimal brain dysfunction in children, Terminology and identification, phase one. U.S. Department of Health, Education and Welfare, NIMB Monogr. 3, January 1966.

others children in special classes because of adjustment problems.

Teachers need to think of children with learning difficulties as comprising a most heterogeneous group, including children who are either hyperactive or hypoactive, bright or of marginal intelligence, unable to move efficiently or gifted in sports and games, able to use language adequately or handicapped in language abilities.

Despite this heterogeneity, much that is discussed in this chapter applies directly to practically every one of these children because they have certain characteristics in common. They all tend to be self-doubting and over-sensitive to criticism or correction because of their previous failures; for the same reason they all tend to have difficulty in social adjustment.

Children with learning difficulties have been described by Gallagher (1966) as suffering from developmental lags or imbalances. These lags may occur in any psychological ability — in sensory-motor functions, language, perception, thought processes, emotional development, and social adjustment — any of which tends to be detrimental to a child's ability to learn. These children may also suffer from global disturbances, or dysfunctions of the general regulation of the nervous system (see Chapter 1). They are often impulsive, perseverative, distractible, disoriented. Others are characterized by a low energy level and hypoactivity.

These disturbances of children with learning difficulties and problems of perceptual and motor control are discussed in detail in this chapter.

Perceptual, Motor, and Adjustment Problems

Perceptual, motor, and adjustment problems occur so often in children with learning difficulties that they have been considered universal symptoms. Careful studies have shown that they are not universal, but that the incidence is high indeed.

An example is a study made by these authors and their associates in a public school district in California. All of the children (374) in the kindergarten classes were given the *Frostig Developmental Test of Visual Perception* (Maslow et al., 1964). The children were also rated by their teachers for motor coordination. Statistical analysis showed that children whose scores fell in the lower 10 to 20 percent on the perceptual test were very likely to be rated as having poor motor coordination. Motor coordination and perceptual problems were strongly related. The relationship between perceptual disturbances and classroom adjustment was even greater.

Rubin and Braun (1968) report that 40 percent of a group of

children who were diagnosed as "maladjusted" showed dysfunction in both cognitive functions (perceptual and intellectual) and motor behavior.

Ayres (1969) found, using Q-technique factor analysis, that her sample of 36 children with educational handicaps showed two major patterns of deficits: (1) auditory, language, and sequencing and (2) postural and bilateral integration.

Appraising Individual Difficulties

Before a fully effective remedial movement education program can be developed for any group of children, it is necessary to analyze carefully each child's deficiencies in the various attributes of movement. For example, the teacher should know that Pat cannot bend forward and touch the ground without bending his knees. He must bend at the waist and knees simultaneously (lack of flexibility); or that Nora cannot raise her legs while lying on her back (weak abdominal muscles); that John cannot throw a ball accurately (probably poor eye-hand coordination); or that Steven cannot perform bilateral asymmetric movements, such as raising his left arm and right leg simultaneously.

As the teacher's experience accumulates while she is teaching movement education, she will become more astute in appraising a child's disabilities and in designing specific exercises to help him. She will ensure that exercises that extend the movement in the hip joints, that strengthen abdominal muscles, that develop eye-hand coordination, and in which a child can practice asymmetric movements are included to help the Pats, Noras, Johns, and Stevens in her class.

Thus the diverse patterns of skills and deficits that characterize children with learning difficulties make it necessary to vary the emphasis of the movement education program to suit individual needs. The preceding suggestions indicate that a specific clinical approach can be carried out even in the context of group training. The following examples demonstrate this point further.

1. Jerry was unable to differentiate between right and left and therefore could not move the appropriate leg or arm according to the teacher's verbal instructions. When the teacher understood the difficulty, she stood directly in front of Jerry, facing the same direction as he, and did the exercise with the group so that Jerry could duplicate her movements.

2. A group of children were asked to jump over a low, taut rope. The teacher adjusted the height of the rope according to each child's

abilities. Betsy could not effect the jump even when the rope was lying on the floor because she involuntarily pulled herself back with her arms whenever she prepared to jump. She could only cross the rope one foot at a time. The teacher therefore suggested that the child fold her arms over her chest before attempting to jump. The youngster then succeeded. When Betsy had used this method for a short time, the teacher helped her to synchronize arm and leg movements by exerting a light pull on her arms as she jumped over the rope. The teacher's assistance in this case consisted of first directing Betsy to anchor those parts of the body that she could not coordinate with the rest, and then in giving active help in synchronizing the parts of the total movement.

3. Mark was a youngster who had great difficulty in catching a ball. The teacher directed the other children to practice catching and throwing in a variety of ways while she worked with Mark individually. She asked Mark to cup his hands, raise them in front, watch closely, and try to catch first a beanbag and then the ball she threw toward his hands. She threw from very close range until Mark had learned to coordinate eye and hand movements sufficiently well to catch the ball.Then the teacher gradually increased the distance.

4. For another child, throwing and catching were even more difficult. The teacher started training these abilities by simply requiring the boy to roll back a ball that she rolled toward him. Then she continued as she did with Mark in example 3.

In each of these cases, the exercise was scaled down to the ability of the individual child, and each youngster was led to greater proficiency by small advances a step at a time. To achieve this purpose, the teacher had to analyze both the movement to be performed and the nature of each child's difficulty. She then had to be prepared to give help or individual demonstrations to enable the children to master the separate elements and then coordinate them.

In all of the preceding exercises, a child may learn to assume the role of the teacher. It is of great benefit to children to learn to help each other.

A teacher may also have to make other adjustments. For instance, because Joe has difficulty in understanding language, the teacher may have to construct her sentences very carefully and talk slowly and distinctly. To enable Willy to remember what she says, she may have to repeat everything twice. To ensure that Lorna does not interfere with the movements of other children, the teacher may have to structure carefully certain aspects of each session. To help Stephen and Max participate, she may have to consistently smile, nod, and use a light touch and many encouraging words. And to ensure that Susan, who is very distractible, will not be tempted to bounce a ball during the time assigned to flexibility exercises, she may have to put equipment that is not needed out of reach of all the children.

Adapting the Program to Emotional and Social Needs

It is necessary to adapt the program to children's emotional and social needs also. The emotional and social development of children with learning difficulties is rarely smooth and undisturbed. As a rule, these children have experienced so much failure and rejection and suffered so much anxiety and self-doubt that their emotional difficulties alone substantially depress their proficiency in learning and adjusting and in moving freely and skillfully.

Movement education can be of the utmost service in furthering the emotional and social development of children with learning difficulties, but only if the teacher plays an active and sensitive role in satisfying the needs of the children. It is quite as important for the teacher to understand a child's emotional reactions as to understand his physical disabilities. The teacher must be alert for every opportunity to help children feel enjoyment and pride in their success in physical activities and to develop awareness and acceptance of others through group activities.

Children with learning difficulties usually need much more support and encouragement than so-called normal children because they do not trust their own ability to succeed (Towne and Joiner, 1968). For such children, pleasure is an especially important ingredient of the movement education program.

Specific ways in which the teacher can use the program to promote emotional well-being are discussed in this chapter. But perhaps none requires more emphasis than the general approach that might be termed the provision of intrinsic reward. The child who *likes* to read becomes engrossed in his reading; the child who *likes* to play becomes engrossed in his play; the child who *likes* movement education will become an ardent participant.

Feelings of well-being and happiness, a desire to create, and a pleasure in pleasing others are likely to occur when movement education is made pleasant. The joy in movement itself, when experiencing success, can eliminate many problems of lack of motor control, behavior disturbances, and distractibility, and it can help children to direct their attention to the task at hand.

Whenever possible, the teacher should avoid forcing a neurologically handicapped child to perform a given task. When the teacher during a movement education session said, "Now, who would like to run S lines (curved lines on the floor) without bumping into the other children?" all but one child said. "I." One little boy said, "No, I don't want to do it." The teacher replied, "Of course. You may rest." After the child had watched the other children; he became upset because he had not worked with them, and he felt that he had failed. He looked embarrassed, seemingly held back his tears, got red in the face, pressed his lips together, and then hid his head in his arms. The teacher went to him and said, "It is very good when children know when to rest. You did fine work today. Next time, when you are not tired, you will run with us." In this way the teacher helped the child to leave school that day without a feeling of failure. During the next session, the little boy attempted the task without coaxing.

By and large, stimuli and activities that are experienced as pleasant are beneficial to a child, while stimuli and activities that are punitive are experienced as unpleasant and are damaging. As Locke wrote (1693), ". . . it must be permitted for children not only to divert themselves, but to do it after their own fashion. . . . For you must never think to set them right, till they can find delight in the practice of laudable things." The emotional reaction of children to their physical education program will generally indicate whether the program satisfies their emotional needs.

Behavior Control Through Control of Movement

Movement education teaches control of movement. Children learn control while waiting in line, in trying to stop their movements at designated points, in staying inside an assigned space during team activities without disturbing the movement of others, and in interacting with others according to the limits of the activity. In performing movement sequences, a child must inhibit movements that are potentially disruptive to himself — for example, he must not permit the intrusion of movements that might disturb his balance while walking across the balance beam or that might foil a jump or cause him to deviate from his course in running a relay race. Moreover, in completing a movement sequence, a child learns to proceed within the limits of a plan.

As all behavior has a motor aspect, such control of movement may lead to improved control of behavior in general. Unfortunately, no research studies are available to prove that the acquisition of controlled movement in the gym or on the playground transfers to

Standing on your head is great fun!

everyday behavior. Clinical experience, however, strongly suggests
that it does. It is at least generally accepted that the behavior and
attitudes that are acquired in one situation are likely to carry over to
others.

There is only meager research that proves that better control of
movement leads to better control of thought, perception, or emotion,
but that this is the case has been the contention expressed in the
literature concerned with body image (Schilder, 1964; Corder,
1965).

Johnson and Fretz (1967) reported that 79 children given basic
neuromotor-perceptual training showed statistically significant gains
over an eight-week period in speed of visual perception, motor performance, and, what is particularly important, showed greater tol-
erance for frustration. Clinical experience at the Frostig Center sup-
ports this evidence. (See also Oliver, 1958).

Self-Control

The measures that help children control movement and general behavior also promote self-control.

Control, whether of specific movements or of general behavior and social attitudes, can probably be made more effective if the teacher repeatedly reminds the children at appropriate moments during the day of their behavior during movement education. In this way, transfer of behavior patterns achieved during movement education is facilitated.

In promoting self-control, it is helpful to provide short rest periods between exciting and lively exercises and to alternate exercises requiring quiet concentration, such as those for developing body awareness, with those involving more rigorous activities.

Cratty and many others believe that physical education sessions with children with learning difficulties should be kept rather quiet to avoid overstimulating the children. Our experience, however, has been that better results are obtained when lively "fun" exercises are alternated with relaxation exercises.

The teacher may use highly stimulating exercises if she takes care to watch that the children feel good about themselves and do not get upset; that stimulating exercises are always followed by relaxing ones; that the children are always aware that they can control their movements and themselves and that it is essentially their responsibility.

Teaching movement education to children with learning difficulties who are above the primary grades requires the same adaptations that are discussed in this chapter. The need for control has to be stressed periodically. The youngsters should be very conscious of the need for smooth, controlled movements in many activities besides exercises, creative movement, and sports.

Social Awareness

Many children with learning difficulties have considerable difficulty in adjusting to social situations. They have to be helped step by step to learn social behavior. Movement education provides an excellent opportunity for this purpose because the intensity and duration of the social and physical contacts of the children can be carefully controlled.

Such children may be given exercises and activities that involve them in working in pairs or in groups, as well as individually. Exercises in which two children hold hands, or in which one gives support to the other (one holding the other's hand as he walks the balance beam, for instance) prepare children for more complicated interaction in dances and group games. Running various paths without colliding with each other is also a good exercise for making children aware of each other.

Group planning and discussion are also helpful. Children should be encouraged to describe what other children do, to point out the merits of their performance, and to praise each other's achievements.

Other Methods of Control

Teachers are probably familiar with two other methods of helping to modify behavior, which are presented here in the context of movement education: (1) conditioning methods recently advocated (rewards and punishment); and (2) stimulus reduction (Strauss and Lehtinen, 1947; Cruickshank et al., 1961).

Rewards

The era during which tangible rewards were strictly avoided seems to have passed. Nowadays the use of extrinsic rewards is a frequently used method of motivating children with learning difficulties, since they often try to avoid learning tasks either because of previous disappointment and failure or because their hyperactivity makes conformity difficult. They frequently need additional incentives.

An extrinsic reward may be a toy or candy or permission to engage in a preferred activity, given either directly or in exchange for a certain number of tokens or checkmarks earned for good work. Care must be taken, however, that such reinforcers are not used as the main or only method of behavior management. Kuypers, Becker, and O'Leary (1968) state that the " . . . token system . . . is simply one tool within the largest set of tools available to the teacher. . . . The full set of equipment is needed to do the job right."

The selection of exercises should assure success, and thus intrinsic rewards for each child in at least some of the tasks. For example, one youngster in a group, Louise, had poor coordination and muscular strength. She performed certain activities much less well than the others in the group. She was unable to gallop or to get up from a sitting position without helping herself with her hands; or to raise her legs from the floor while lying on her back, even when her shoulders were held down. Realizing that Louise was an imaginative little girl, however, the teacher capitalized on this strength by asking the children to "find a new way of crossing the room" while keeping contact with the floor with three points of the body (one hand and both feet, for instance). In tasks like this, which gave Louise scope for her creativity, she usually thought of more variations than any other child, and she received due admiration.

As a rule, the teacher should not force a child to attempt something that he is afraid to do or is unlikely to succeed in. She should find a task with which the child feels comfortable and then build in small steps toward the more demanding task so as to prevent, if possible, fear or failure.

Children with learning difficulties have one common overwhelming need — to feel better about themselves. The best reward for most of them is, therefore, success, reinforced by a social reward, such as praise, a smile, a nod, or any other form of friendly behavior on the part of the teacher and classmates.

Punishment

Punishment should not play a major role in the management of children. Although a child may pay attention most easily to punishment, such as loud noises, pain, or deprivation of pleasure, the gain in attention is achieved at great cost to the child. The tension and stress that result tend to disturb the child's total development rather than promote it.

It is certainly a damaging procedure to use such punishment as shaking, shouting, or hitting. But even the milder forms of punishment, such as scolding or depriving of pleasure (by restricting the play period, for example), should be avoided as regular procedure.

It is possible to control certain behavior by systematic punishment, but it is doubtful if control achieved in this way carries over to other situations.* Pleasant stimuli may be less commanding, but they are more effective.

Stimulus Reduction

It is possible to reduce distracting stimuli in movement education, although only to a degree.

The behavior of hyperactive children can be helped by interpolating relaxation exercises (see Chapters 4 and 12) in the movement education period. Temporary exclusion of stimuli, such as having the children lie on the floor in relaxed positions with eyes closed, is most helpful. We have also seen excellent results when quiet music was played while the children were resting after exercise. Even better results are obtained if a relaxation or breathing exercise precedes complete rest.

We strongly suggest that whenever the teacher works either with a class of children with learning difficulties or has such children in her regular classroom that the movement education lesson end on a quiet note.

It is also wise to put equipment away and out of reach when it is not in immediate use. If not, restless Johnny may continue to

---

*Reese (1967) states, "The laboratory evidence to date indicates that unless very severe intensities are used, aversive stimulation alone does not suppress behavior permanently."

throw beanbags in the air instead of lining up for an exercise on the balance beam.

The children should also be prevented as far as possible from distracting each other by untimely actions or talking not related to their activities.

Maintaining Optimum Tension Levels

Many children with learning difficulties cannot deal with certain levels of tension and stress. If the tension is too high, one child may "go to pieces" and exhibit what Goldstein (1948) terms a "catastrophic reaction." On the other hand, if the tension is too low, another child may become sluggish, listless, bored, and inattentive.

In the classroom, Sarah, for example, who was anxious and physically weak, required a slow pace and much rest, but she experienced mild stimulation as pleasant. She needed a medium tension level. Jonas, on the other hand, was usually tense, showed poorly controlled, rapid movements, and easily became overexcited. He needed a very low tension level, with frequent periods in which he could release his energy, followed by rest.

While both Sarah and Jonas showed disorganized behavior when overstimulated, the activities that produced a calming effect were different for both of them. Sarah was calmed by a pleasant, mildly elating experience, such as quiet mimetic play with a doll. Jonas needed to punch the punching bag until he became tired and then to rest quietly while he simmered down. By contrast, another child might have a tension level so low that he would fall asleep if he were not kept alert and motivated by every possible means, such as rewards for achievement and the repeated stimulation of sounds, words, and physical contact.

In the classroom, the teacher must help the children directly in maintaining an optimum tension level. It is usually necessary for her to suggest and to guide the children in shifting to appropriate activities. In addition, suitable materials, such as dolls and punching bags, should always be available.

Our experience has shown, however, that during the movement education period, after the first two or three sessions, most of the regulation of tension and tempo is done by the children themselves — if the teacher varies the activities and gauges the overall tempo to the general level of the group and if each child feels successful. Children will exert themselves to varying degrees. The teacher should encourage a child to rest if he wants to. Such self-regulation is an essential part of self-control, as discussed above.

Awareness of Time, Space, and Causality

Movement education promotes children's awareness — awareness of environment, of time, of space, and of causality. To adjust the time of reaction in responding to a stimulus — to avoid short-circuiting through immediate reaction or to avoid getting into danger because of an inability to adjust the tempo of movement to the task — requires cognition of time, space, and causality. Such cognition is an indispensable factor in learning control of movement.

Objects and events are perceived as occurring in time and space and being connected with each other. But many children with learning difficulties have disturbed awareness of time, space, and causality; it is jumbled, fluid, and incoherent. When this awareness is disturbed, perception of reality is disturbed also. As a result, overt behavior also becomes disorganized.

Time

Without a sense of time, a child feels confused, for his life seems to lack unity and predictability. Moreover, his lack of sense of time may bring him into conflict with his environment by causing him to arrive too late or too early for the convenience of others or to want meals at odd hours, for instance. Academic progress can also be seriously affected. Bateman (1968) states: "It is evident that temporal disabilities are involved in many kinds of educational difficulties. Specific areas mentioned included spelling, writing, reading, speech and language, and rhythmic difficulties. . . ."*

The skills mentioned by Bateman involve the ability to pay attention to successive events. Awareness of time and awareness of sequences are reciprocal processes. Awareness of the flow of time is experienced only through the change of events, and it is generally poorly perceived by children whose attention wanders or who are only dimly aware of their surroundings. It can easily be understood that difficulties in academic work must result.

Space

Space is perceived as an extension of one's own body. Body awareness is so important, both for space perception and for self-concept, that Chapter 4 is devoted to this topic.

Poor spatial awareness is often combined with a deficiency in body awareness. Clinical observations, however, indicate that difficulties in awareness of spatial relationships also occur in some chil-

*Used by permission of the author and publisher.

dren with relatively intact body awareness. Such children get around quite well as long as there is nothing in their way. In such cases, the clumsiness may be the result of visual perceptual difficulties, and testing and training in visual perception should be instituted. Or the clumsiness may be the result of lack of attention to the environment, and the cause of such inattention, including preoccupation caused by emotional problems, needs to be explored.

Piaget (1954, 1956, 1962) has shown that the early sensory-motor activities of a child (his play, the movements he engages in while playing, and the observation of the effect of these movements) affect the subsequent development of his cognitive functions and understanding. In experiencing movement, a child can experience time, space, and the logic of events, and thus learn to make sense of his environment and gain a firmer apprehension of reality. The teacher can structure and conduct the movement education program in such a way as to facilitate this process.

Structuring Time and Space

The importance of structure for the education of children with learning difficulties is mentioned in almost all writings about the education of such children. Structuring a task refers to relating the different aspects of a task to each other or relating subsequent tasks to each other (Bruner, 1966).

To learn a movement sequence, which involves time and space, a child must first attend to the instructions. Then he must keep the total sequence in mind while attending to each detail in the right order. This is frequently most difficult for children with learning disabilities, who, besides their problems of perception of temporal, spatial, and causal sequences, may be unable to remember these sequences for more than short periods of time. As a result they have difficulty in grasping and reproducing movements and sequences.

The "wholes" that children with learning handicaps can grasp are small; they must be built up bit by bit to form larger "wholes" (Drowatsky, 1965).

The teacher can structure an exercise or movement sequence by clarifying the temporal, spatial, and causal relationships of the task step by step. Learning to run a relay race, for example, can be structured step by step. The teacher first shows the children where each should stand in line, thus making them aware of spatial relationships. She might then suggest the following as an introductory game: "When I say 'Run!' you run to your places. See if you can get there before I repeat the word 'run' four times. It will sound like this: 'Run . . . run . . . run . . . run!' All ready? Run . . . run . . . run . . .

run . . . !' " In waiting for the signal, running immediately after hearing it, and in keeping track of the number of times the word "run" is said, the children learn to perceive temporal sequences and time span.

After the children have learned to run to a goal, the teacher should ask them to take turns in walking to a designated place on a given signal, pick up a beanbag, and return to the end of the line, handing the beanbag in passing to the child at the front of the line. Finally, the children repeat the sequence as a relay race, but running instead of walking. In such a step-by-step sequence, the temporal relationships can be emphasized by telling the children, "*First* you do this, *then* you do this, *finally* you do this." The spatial relationships can be emphasized by pointing out, "You go from your place to the goal, then back to the first child in line, and then to the end of the line."

The teacher may, however, have to divide the task into further steps for some children — for example, it might be necessary to teach the children how to hand the beanbag to the next child.

Children with learning difficulties should be required to overlearn each segment of an activity through repetition until they can complete the entire sequence without mistake. Clinical experience indicates that many children otherwise unable to reproduce movement sequences are helped if they are able to observe them repeatedly, as well as experience them. They should, therefore, have ample opportunity to observe the teacher and each other. Teaching all of the steps of an exercise, such as the relay race, may take days or even weeks, but the children will learn in this way to engage in sequential behavior and become more aware of time, space, and causality.

Structured movement exercises should be presented verbally, pictorially, and in writing:

For young children, the oral and written instructions might be:
1. Stand straight.
2. When I clap, run to the gate.
3. Run back.

For older children, the instructions might be:

1. Hands and feet on the floor like a dog.
2. Hands off the floor, weight on legs.
3. Stand straight.
4. Bend knees and stretch arms forward.
5. Be a "dog" again.
6. Repeat three times.

Cratty (1963) has recommended the following four steps in teaching movement sequences to children with learning difficulties.

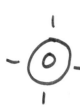

1. The teacher should attempt to determine the capacity of a pupil to perceptually organize the whole movement sequence.
2. The *whole* movement should be related to a similar movement with which the learner may be familiar.
3. The *whole* movement should then be taught, or as much of the whole as has been determined the learner can perceptually assimilate.
4. Upon obtaining a general perception of the entire "schema" of the movement, the learner should then be guided to correct the "schema" until the action resembles the one desired by the teacher and the learner.

Following is an example of the use of Cratty's four steps:

1. Child A, who was well coordinated, was told to gallop around the playground while the other children watched. Then the teacher asked all the children to gallop.

2. A few children had difficulties with galloping. The teacher asked these children to remember how they had learned to jump over a rope on the previous day, raising high first *one* knee and then the other.

3. The teacher then asked the children to pretend to jump over a rope in the same way.

4. The teacher then asked the children to take one step and pull up their knees at each step. After the children had learned to gallop, the teacher helped them to perform the movement sequence more

smoothly by suggesting further adjustments, such as raising the knees higher and moving faster.

Such spatial and temporal structuring, especially when frequently verbalized by both teacher and child, is most helpful in making children aware of sequences in time and space and of cause and effect. It is an important aid to ameliorating global disturbances because it helps children to formulate and internalize a plan of action, to learn it, to execute it, and to repeat it.

Other Methods of Developing Awareness of Time and Space

The example above shows how the steps in a relay race can be taught in such a way as to promote both temporal and spatial awareness. But awareness of time and space may also be influenced by many activities designed to establish order during movement education: showing the children where the equipment is, where they are to stand, how to line up, where their places are during exercises, the position they have to adopt in relation to a piece of equipment (in front, behind, or to the side), and their position in relation to other children. They should become aware of the necessary sequence of their activities — setting up equipment first and in a certain order, doing the exercise in the correct sequence, taking the equipment down, and putting it away.

Temporal and spatial awareness is also learned by body movement — by making a running step to gain momentum for a jump or by raising the hips off the floor to get up to a shoulder stand, for example.

Children may also be made aware of time by the use of rhythm.* Disorganized children are usually arrhythmic (Doll, 1951). Seeing and performing rhythmic movements, whether in the form of exercises or dances or relays, with or without the accompaniment of percussion instruments or music, help children to become aware of temporal structure.

Awareness of time may also be improved by using a stopwatch or hourglass so that the children find out how long an activity lasts and from learning to tell time. It is necessary for children to be aware of speed (the slowness or quickness of movement) if they are to be able to perceive time intervals.

In general, if an activity is planned carefully, taught in a step-by-step manner, and verbalized after it is executed, a child will develop

---

*Webster's Second International Dictionary defines rhythm as "Movement marked by regular recurrence of, or regular alternation in, features, elements, phenomena, etc.; hence regularity of recurrence or alternation, or an instance of it; periodicity."

an inner "reliving" of a sequence, which is necessary to perceive time and remember the connectedness of events.

Spatial awareness is promoted as a child learns to master his body in space, to achieve free movement, and to intercept or avoid other objects, such as throwing and catching a ball, jumping over a rope, hitting a tetherball, running through a rolling hoop, or negotiating an obstacle course.

The teacher must take into account, however, that children who lack spatial awareness may be afraid of hurting themselves or making others angry or scornful by their ineptitude. If this anxiety is not allayed, it may cause them to perform even more clumsily or avoid movement altogether. It is sometimes possible to help a child to overcome his anxiety by teaching him a simple stunt or dance that he can perform with pride. It is in any case essential to begin with very easy tasks and to provide much praise and encouragement.

While teaching the skills essential for spatial awareness, the teacher should take the opportunity of teaching spatial concepts, such as *above, below, down, up, right, left, middle,* and *in front.*

As in the promotion of time awareness, verbalization by teacher and children, as well as visualization and auditorization (making a mental picture and hearing the auditory sequence in one's mind), is of greatest importance.

A child's awareness of the relationship of his body to the surrounding space influences his movement patterns. This aspect of training is discussed in Chapter 5.

Influencing the Tempo of Movement

Hyperactive Children

The most frequent deviation from the norm in regard to the tempo, as well as the frequency, of movement is hyperactivity. Hyperactive children are in continuous motion. The movements are usually quite jerky, hasty, abrupt, and not goal directed, often interfering with the completion of their own tasks and the tasks of others. Slow, accurate movements, which require careful guidance by kinesthesia, vision, and listening, are difficult for these children. They tend to spill things at the table; to trip over their shoelaces, which they cannot tie; to bump and shove other children unintentionally; and to be inaccurate in following commands. They have difficulty in integrating motor acts, language, and perceptions. In learning to count, for example, they cannot point accurately at objects while saying the number; they tend to skip items. (See Chapter 7.)

In learning movement sequences, such as simple dance steps, they are handicapped because of their inability to slow down their movements. In other school tasks, they make many apparently careless mistakes, such as copying incorrectly, following directions incorrectly, or writing answers to problems in wrong spaces either because they are lagging in spatial perception or because they do not take the necessary time to orient themselves and plan their actions before plunging into the task.

Movement education provides many opportunities for controlling hyperactivity. Hyperactive children improve if the teacher helps them to plan their movements before they execute them, makes them pause and think before they act, slows down hasty reactions by verbal intervention, and makes sure that they execute tasks in the order learned. The injunction to "think first and act afterwards" needs constant repetition.

Hypoactive Children

Hypoactivity is less frequently observed and described. Hypoactive children move slowly, sit motionless for long periods of time, show low energy levels, need a time lapse before they can react to a command, and lag behind their group in the execution of tasks.

Hypoactivity is more resistant to treatment than hyperactivity. Nevertheless, treatment is usually helpful, although it may be a lengthy process. The authors' clinical experience at the Frostig Center indicates that children who are hypoactive are enabled to speed up their actions and reactions through much practice, but that they often need treatment far into adolescence. They need to be made aware of their own slowness and also that with practice they can improve.

Children who are hypoactive have to be treated with great patience. The teacher must not expect too much of them, nor must they expect too much of themselves. The teacher must help such children to speed up their reactions by tiny increments. They should also be helped to increase the speed of on-going movements, such as running, and should practice agility exercises in which they have to change body position while in motion. With such children, the teacher may need to use stronger stimuli than usual, varying her voice level and injecting admonishments. The use of a clock, egg timer, or metronome may be helpful in accelerating the tempo of movements.

The teacher needs to realize, however, that these children cannot compete with others but only with themselves. Any gain, however small, must be immediately acknowledged and praised, even though a child may still seem to move in slow motion compared with his classmates.

Planning the Level and Sequence of Activities

One of the most important aspects in adapting the movement education program for children with learning difficulties is the frequent necessity of starting with simple, basic exercises.

In a group of nine children six and seven years old, there were several who were unable to execute the simplest movement or command, such as take one step forward. Instead they took two steps or took one step sideways or backward. When asked to raise a knee they raised a foot. These children had to be taught to direct their bodies in simple movements, and in some cases a child's arm or head, for instance, had to be moved by the teacher before the child could initiate the movement himself.

The first exercises in this book (Chapter 4) are designed primarily to help children with the execution of simple tasks that depend on awareness of the body. A child must learn to raise an arm or a leg at will, to bend a knee, or to move his trunk in a given direction. Nearly all children improve quickly when such simple movements are taught carefully. Within the first few lessons, children who have been unable to follow simple directions learn to execute two or three movements at the same time; for example, to jump forward and raise their arms at the same time. The children become aware of their new-found ability to regulate the movements of their bodies, and they express their pleasure concerning their achievements.

Although it is important for all children to have an optimum self-concept, it is especially important for children with learning difficulties. These children feel impotent, lost, and unable to do things that other children can do. They frequently ask for reassurance with such questions as "Can I get to the top of the jungle gym?" "Do you think I can stand on my hands?" "Do you think I can walk in a straight line?"

When the children make positive statements, such as "I can walk an S line on the floor," or "I can walk a circle on the floor," or "I can put my leg forward, and I can make my hands go up very high," the teacher knows that she is pacing the program correctly.

To help very young children become aware that they can master new skills, a game such as the following may be used. The children form a circle (or several circles if there are more than ten in the class) and while walking sing, "We are all so proud of Julie (or John, or whomever) because Julie can turn around" (or whatever it is Julie can do). The game can be played either by the teacher giving directions to the children or by the children thinking of movements

SOCIAL

POSIT.
REIN.
FOR SELF CONCEPT

When a pair of children learn to work together they can jump from board to board with coordination.

themselves. But the teacher should be careful to introduce some new movements so that the children enlarge their movement repertoires and can then demonstrate that they have learned something new.

In classes of children with learning difficulties there are always some who improve more slowly than others. Such children should get more help, and they should know that the teacher appreciates any effort and any progress, even if it is small. One exceedingly clumsy youngster in a group of children ten to thirteen years of age could not weave back and forth between the rungs of the jungle gym. He finally was able to crawl between two rungs to the other side. He was delighted with his success and received lavish praise from the teacher, although he could not reach the other children's level of accomplishment.

The pace in introducing more difficult exercises must be slow in the beginning because the children need a great deal of individual help. During the first sessions they should observe each other and the teacher's movements and learn from each other. (Later they should be more active.) This is important because research shows clearly that observation of movement in learning movement skills is as important as practicing movement itself. Children become actively involved not only when they move themselves but also when they observe and later reproduce what they have observed. Children should therefore watch how the teacher and another child take a step forward or make a turn or whatever else they do.

The teacher should always ask the children who are able to do a certain movement to show it to the other children. But she must structure the lesson so that each child is able to demonstrate something to the others and thus feel that he is at times a leader.

Directing Attention

Watching the teacher's or another child's movement is also helpful because it requires the children's attention. Directing attention is so very difficult for many children, and it is so necessary for them to learn.

Helping children to pay attention is discussed in several places in this book. One method of special importance meriting repetition is the use of forewarning, or conditional command, such as *"When I clap my hands, then you jump up,"* or "Wait until I say *'now'!"*

Laterality and Directionality

Observers of children with learning difficulties have noted frequent occurrences of lack of hand dominance and recognition of left and right, as well as disabilities in motor functions and perceptions. Much has been written concerning the interrelationship of these functions and their relationship to neurological organization, but differences of opinion still persist.

Laterality and directionality, as well as exercises to establish awareness of right and left and direction in space, are discussed in Chapter 4. They are mentioned again here, however, because children with learning difficulties frequently have problems with directionality.

Language

The role that thoughtful use of language can play in helping children with learning difficulties has been demonstrated previously in this chapter, as well as in Chapter 6. The appropriate use of such words as *fast* and *slow, sooner* and *later, before* and *after* helps children to become aware of time. The use of such words as *tall* and *short, narrow* and *wide* helps children to become aware of space and of the spatial characteristics of objects.

The teacher should use the words herself and encourage the children to use them appropriately. The careful verbalization of each procedure in a movement sequence helps children to acquire temporal and spatial concepts. It also helps them to develop the use of inner language, which enables them to control their own behavior, analyze tasks, and perform them in the right order. Inner language is also developed when a child is asked to describe an activity that he has already performed. To continue the illustration of teaching a relay race, a child could, for example, say after carrying out the sequence: "I was standing still at the red line until the teacher gave a signal. Then as soon as I heard the whistle, I started to run. I ran to the yellow post where John held out the beanbag. I took the beanbag, and I ran back and gave it to Jack. Then I ran to the end of the line." Later on, the child learns to repeat a sequence in his mind only.

Caution must be exercised concerning too frequent verbalization *before* a sequence is carried out, however. The ability to imitate or to plan and carry out movement sequences precedes verbalization in the normal child. Verbalization becomes the facilitator for many actions subsequently. But learning solely through visual, tactile, and kinesthetic channels retains its importance, especially with regard to kinesthetic stimuli, which are so important for the development of body awareness. Verbal communication should thus be minimized at times, and a child should be allowed to express himself in the language of the body — to perceive, to visualize, and to schematize movement sequences without the aid of words. Both kinds of learning should be used.

In the use of language in teaching movement education to children with learning difficulties, the teacher needs to bear in mind the likelihood that some children have limited ability to use or to understand language (Drowatsky, 1965).

It may be necessary to give verbal explanations and instructions briefly and very simply and to repeat them often. It is sometimes difficult to decide whether a child fails to give a correct response because the task is too difficult for him, because he balks for some reason, or because he cannot understand the directions. It is advisable, therefore, whenever a child's response is not correct, to rephrase the directions immediately, simplifying them. It is worth remembering that children react easier to commands telling them *what* to do than to those telling them *what not* to do. If a child does not respond to a direction, such as "John, stop playing tetherball," the teacher might try a simpler positive command, such as "John, come to me."

Suggestions are given in Chapter 6 for using movement education to provide language development.

Works Cited

Ayres, A. J. Deficits in sensory integration in educationally handicapped children. *Journal of Learning Disabilities,* 1969, 2 (3), 160-168.

Barsch, R. H. *A Movigenic Curriculum.* Bulletin No. 25, Bureau of Handicapped Children. Madison, Wis.: State Department of Public Instruction, 1965.

Bateman, B. *Temporal Learning.* (Dimensions in Early Learning Series.) San Rafael, Calif.: Dimensions Publishing, 1968.

Bruner, J. S. *Toward a Theory of Instruction.* Cambridge, Mass.: Harvard Univ. Press, 1966.

Clements, S. D. *Minimal Brain Dysfunction in Children: Terminology and Identification, Phase One.* U. S. Department of Health, Education and Welfare, NIMB, Monogr. 3, January 1966.

Corder, W. O. Effects of physical education on the intellectual, physical, and social development of educable mentally retarded boys. Unpublished doctoral dissertation, Department of Special Education, George Peabody College for Teachers, June 1965.

Cratty, B. J. Schema with correction and motor learning. *Physical Educator,* 1963, 20 (1), 23-24.

Cruickshank, W. M., Bentzen, F. A., Ratzeburg, F. H., and Tannhauser, M. T. *A Training Method for Brain-Injured and Hyperactive Children.* Special Education and Rehabilitation Monogr. Series No. 6. Syracuse, N.Y.: Syracuse Univ. Press, 1961.

Doll, E. Education and the interjacent child. Address at the fifth anniversary of The Vanguard School, Haverford, Pa., January 30, 1965.

Doll, E. Neurophrenia. *American Journal of Psychiatry,* 1951, 108, 50-53.

Drowatsky, J. N. Physical education for the brain-damaged child. *Physical Educator*, 1965, 2 (2), 76-77.

Gallagher, J. Children with developmental imbalances: A psychoeducational definition. In W. M. Cruickshank (Ed.), *The Teacher of Brain-Injured Children.* Special Education and Rehabilitation Monogr. Series No. 7. Syracuse, N.Y.: Syracuse Univ. Press, 1966.

Goldstein, K. *Language and Language Disturbances.* New York: Grune & Stratton, 1948.

Johnson, W. R., and Fretz, B. R. Developmental and therapeutic values of physical play and sport for children. In *Sport Psychology: A Symposium.* Sofia, Bulgaria: State Publishing House of Sport Medicine, 1967.

Kephart, N. C. *The Slow Learner in the Classroom.* Columbus, Ohio: Charles E. Merrill, 1960.

Kuypers, D. S., Becker, W. C., and O'Leary, K. D.   How to make a token system fail. *Exceptional Children,* 1968, **35** (2), 101-108.

Locke, J. *Some Thoughts Concerning Education.* Woodbury, N.Y.: Barron, 1965. (First printed 1693.)

Maslow, P., Frostig, M., Lefever, D. W., and Whittlesey, J. R. B. The Marianne Frostig developmental test of visual perception, 1963 standardization. *Perceptual and Motor Skills,* 1964, **19**, 463-499. (Monogr. Suppl. 2-V19.)

Naville, S., and Ajuriaguerra, J. H. Rééducation psychomotrice. *Revue Belge de Therapeutique Physique,* 1967, **34**, 3-14.

Oliver, J. N. The effect of physical conditioning exercises and activities on the mental characteristics of educationally sub-normal boys. *British Journal of Educational Psychology, 1958.* **28**, 155-165.

Piaget, J. *The Construction of Reality in the Child.* New York: Basic Books, 1954.

Piaget, J. *The Origins of Intelligence in Children.* New York: International Universities Press, 1956.

Piaget, J. *Play, Dreams and Imitation in Childhood.* New York: W. W. Norton, 1962.

Reese, E. P. *The Analysis of Human Operant Behavior.* Dubuque, Iowa: W. C. Brown, 1967.

Rubin, E. C., and Braun, J. B. Behavioral and learning disabilities associated with cognitive-motor dysfunction. *Perceptual and Motor Skills,* 1968, **26**, 171-180.

Schilder, P. *The Image and Appearance of the Human Body.* New York: John Wiley, 1964. (First published in English, 1950.)

Strauss, A. A., and Lehtinen, L. E. *Psychopathology and Education of the Brain-Injured Child.* Vol. 1. New York: Grune & Stratton, 1947.

Towne, R. C., and Joiner, L. M. Some negative implications of special placement for children with learning disabilities. *Journal of Special Education,* 1968, **2** (2), 217-222.

Facilities, Equipment, and Management of Movement Education

Planning of the movement education program in any school is influenced by the indoor and outdoor facilities available, by weather, and by state time requirements.

Recommended Time

State law or state regulation governs the minimum amount of time used for physical education in many schools. We, however, recommend the following minimum times for this program on the basis of age, grade, and children's needs and abilities (not including time for changing shoes or clothes):

Kindergarten — 20 to 25 minutes daily; 1 hour, 40 minutes weekly.

Grades 1 through 3 — 30 to 35 minutes daily; 2-1/2 hours weekly.

If the gymnasium and playground are not available on certain days, the teacher should have at least two 5- to 10-minute exercise periods in the classroom on those days.

Teaching in the Classroom

Movement skills are so important that movement education should be an integral part of the daily curriculum, however inadequate the facilities and however cold or wet the weather may be.

If facilities are inadequate or the weather poor, this program can be adapted to the space available. The teacher who has a gymnasium at her disposal only two days a week, for instance, should not abandon movement education on the other three days because the playground is wet or covered with snow or because there is a conflict with another class in the use of the playground or gymnasium. She may conduct the program in the classroom.

Adjusting the program to the classroom means more restriction in certain phases than in others. Creative movement (Chapter 5), for example, requires considerable space, whether on a playground or in a

153

gymnasium, because creative movement is largely based on children's encounters with space. Exercises that require running to a goal, throwing balls and other objects, and group circle games also require a great deal of space.

Nevertheless, the teacher who has only a classroom to work in can substitute running on the spot or in the aisles for running to a goal. A running broad jump may be replaced by a standing broad jump in the area in front of the teacher's desk, and exercises that normally require a lying position* may be replaced by those requiring a sitting position. The teacher must select the exercises that can be done in the space at her disposal.

Spatial restrictions inevitably lead to time restrictions. Children who have to exercise in a small space become tired and bored more easily than children who have the use of a playground or gym. In such cases, the teacher may have to reduce an exercise period to 5 to 10 minutes. She can, however, maintain the recommended total time each day by conducting two or three sessions a day.

Innumerable examples bear out the value of frequent short sessions of movement education, and we should like to attest to the value by describing an example we read about. A sixth-grade class of underprivileged children in metropolitan New York were hostile, inattentive, fidgety, and refused to learn. Observing their restlessness, the teacher concluded that the children's need for exercise was not being met; that they needed activity to channel their emotions. He decided to give them a 10-minute break every hour during which they could play games. This proved to be his first step to success in teaching his class.

If space is cramped, music may accompany the exercises more often than usual to restore some of the joy and zest denied by the lack of free movement. Drums, tambourines, maracas, bells, and records or tape recordings may be used. Where open space or a gymnasium is available, however, music should be limited to a small part of the lessons so that each child develops his own rhythm and style and finds the tempo most suitable for his individual constitution and body makeup.

Playground Design

The best place for primary school movement education is a playground — a playground with a grassy area. Turf is infinitely preferable to a hard surface playground. There should, however, also be an all-

---

*Inexpensive mats of plastic or straw may be used in the classroom.

weather blacktop area on which number lines and other markings may be painted (see Chapters 6 and 8).

In urban areas particularly the playground should approach the natural as much as possible so that teachers and children alike can develop the delight in nature and respect for beauty that are unfortunately so often lacking. It is sad to realize that some children in cities rarely see even a tree. Playgrounds should not, therefore, be bare, but should at least have some trees, shrubs, and plants grown in containers if no ground plots are available. Movable foliage provides objects for obstacle runs, as well as refreshment for the eye and lessons in nature study.

If possible, a small area should be available for gardening, as planting and nurturing plants not only afford a great deal of physical exercise, but they also establish a valuable contact with nature. Plants are frequently not planted on playgrounds because it is thought that they take up too much space and that children destroy them. But plants can form natural barriers, occupying little playing space, and we have observed that even the most violent youngsters become tender when handling seedlings and growing plants. A youngster's pride in an attractive playground and in plants nurtured by himself enriches his life and contributes greatly to his development as a human being with a capacity for love and a sense of responsibility for living things.

Playground designs, of course, vary according to the funds and space available and to the climate. The drawing below shows how careful planning can make the most of a very small space by using the middle of the playground for activities for which marks on the ground are required and arranging the equipment around the periphery.

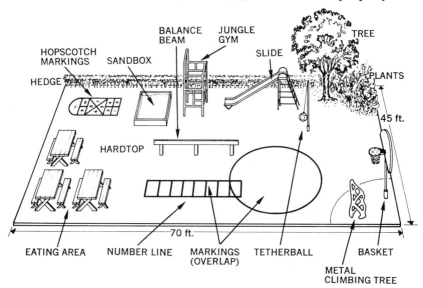

BALANCE BEAM JUNGLE GYM SLIDE TREE

HOPSCOTCH MARKINGS SANDBOX PLANTS

HEDGE 45 ft.

HARDTOP

70 ft.

EATING AREA   NUMBER LINE   MARKINGS (OVERLAP)   TETHERBALL   BASKET

METAL CLIMBING TREE

The pieces of equipment should be so spaced that they can be used either individually or together for an obstacle course. An obstacle course is desirable because it can be used to help develop all the attributes of movement. At the same time, the pieces should be sufficiently far apart so that different groups of children can work on them separately but simultaneously. In the Cupertino, California, playground illustrated on page 158, one group, for example, might be trying different ways of proceeding between the tires on the ground — jumping on one foot, jumping on two feet, turning in the air while jumping. Another group might be swinging from the suspended ropes, assuming different body positions as they do so; another group might be climbing the stile or walking along the tree trunks in various ways. The children thus use different pieces of equipment simultaneously without waiting for or interfering with each other.

The middle of the playground, without equipment, can meanwhile be used for exercises and for creative movement.

Equipment

Movement education can be conducted without apparatus, but the use of it enhances teamwork, focuses attention, trains coordination, agility, flexibility, and balance, and it gives children a wonderful sense of mastery.

It is not essential to have a great deal of stationary or portable equipment, but the playground should be equipped for young children with at least sufficient apparatus for climbing, jumping, balancing, and crawling. In a climate such as that in California, outdoor movement education facilities are used more often than they are in colder climates. The equipment should, therefore, include more apparatus to be used under the direction of the teacher, such as vertical and horizontal ladders, and less equipment for recreation, such as swings, teeter-totters, and merry-go-rounds.

Some playground equipment comes as a package. Examples are the "Playscapes," which are colorful and esthetically pleasing, need relatively little room, and provide much climbing apparatus. Equipment has also recently been devised that may be taken apart and put together in a variety of ways, which saves space and permits children to create their own combinations. An example is the stegel.

Following is a list of recommended, but not required, equipment:

Jungle gym or other climbing equipment,* preferably including a tree. Small jungle gyms can be used by preschoolers for climbing. Older children need larger structures that allow them to twist, turn, and tumble. The ground or mats may also be used for tumbling activities.

Balance beam or log for balance exercises. A 2-inch by 4-inch board 6 to 12 feet long supported by posts at both ends is common. Beginners should use the 4-inch surface and progress to the 2-inch surface. Benches may also be used for balance exercises.

Balance board for balance exercises. The balance board is a square platform with a center post. Three-inch, four-inch, and five-inch posts are commonly provided. Beginners and children who have difficulty with balance should start with the five-inch post. (Many educators believe a balance board is "must" equipment, but we consider it optional. Many exercises for balance that do not require a balance board are included in Chapter 12.)

Trampoline or trampoline board. A trampoline board† should be available whenever there is insufficient space or funds for a trampoline. It is smaller (measuring about 6 feet by 16 inches) than a trampoline. Although it is less versatile than a trampoline, it has its advantages. It is lightweight and takes up little room. Trampolines and trampoline boards stimulate children to jump in an endless variety of styles and patterns, the flying sensation they impart is immensely stimulating and satisfying, and they are most effective in promoting body awareness.

Swings or other apparatus for rhythmic movement of the whole body. Circular slides and teeter-totters serve the same purpose. If no commercial equipment is available, tires hung by ropes will serve.

Slides.

Sandbox.

Improvising equipment from tires, boards, pipes, and other materials can stimulate creativity and provide a great deal of fun. Drawings of two playgrounds equipped inexpensively are shown on pages 158 and 159. The playgrounds were designed and equipped according to the authors' suggestions by the Cupertino, California, School District, which was intent upon providing the most efficient facilities at the least expense. The materials — wooden poles, ropes,

---

*There are many commercially available pieces of equipment that may be used for climbing. Many of these may be used in varying ways to encourage creative movement on the part of children. Among these are the "Play Tree" and the "Play Wall" (Jamison, Inc., 19253 South Vermont Ave., Torrance, Calif.) and the "Obstacle Climber" (J. E. Burke Co., P.O. Box 549, Fond du Lac, Wis. 54935).

†One source for these trampoline boards is Perception Development Research Associates, P.O. Box 936, La Porte, Texas 77571.

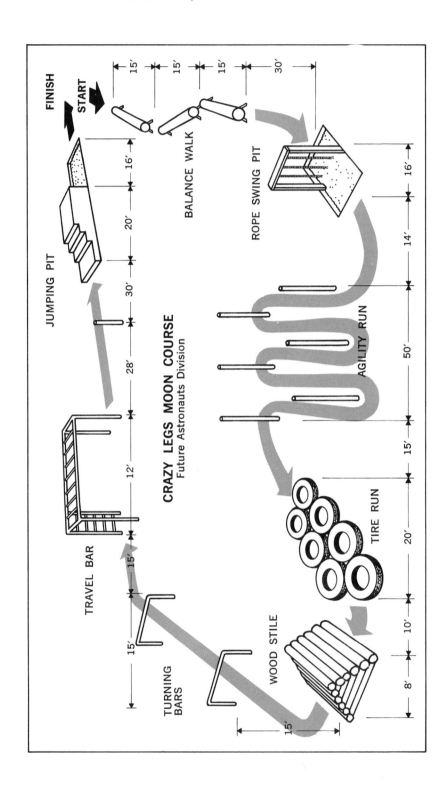

FINISH

START

15' 15' 15' 30'

BALANCE WALK

ROPE SWING PIT

JUMPING PIT

16'

20'

30'

28'

12'

16'

14'

50'

15'

CRAZY LEGS MOON COURSE
Future Astronauts Division

AGILITY RUN

TRAVEL BAR

15'

TIRE RUN

20'

10'

8'

TURNING BARS

15'

WOOD STILE

15'

15'

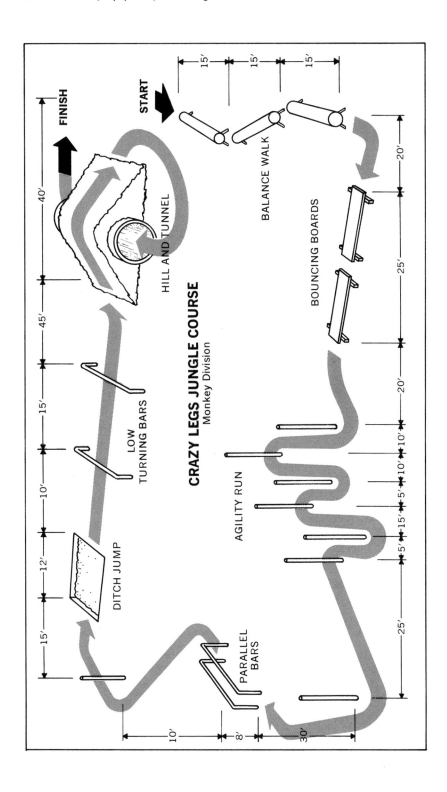

CRAZY LEGS JUNGLE COURSE
Monkey Division

START

FINISH

BALANCE WALK

HILL AND TUNNEL

BOUNCING BOARDS

LOW TURNING BARS

AGILITY RUN

DITCH JUMP

PARALLEL BARS

and a few pipes for climbing, turning, and vaulting — are easily obtainable.

We do not mean to suggest that all playgrounds should be constructed with a minimum of expenditure. But self-made equipment has advantages besides economy: it is warmer and friendlier because less metal is used than in most commercial playground equipment; it can unite a group of parents who might enjoy building playground equipment; it leaves more room for children's imaginations to work.

On the other hand, good commercial playground equipment has great advantages. It is usually more durable, more complex (offering opportunities for more forms of physical exercise), more attractively designed, and more colorful. The two latter considerations are important, for playgrounds should be as attractive as possible to offset the dreary environment in which so many children live.

Children may give different names to a playground at different times, and they may use it for different imaginative games. The equipment can also represent different objects from time to time, such as houses, rockets, trees, bridges, cars, trains, spacecraft, stockades, drawbridges, and planets. The children should learn to use each item of equipment in a variety of ways and to think about new ways of using each.

Even if all the equipment desired or recommended is not available, a complete and well-balanced movement education program can be carried out with a few pieces of movable equipment and such supplies as ropes, balls, beanbags, and lines and markings on the ground (Rasmus, 1968).

Markings

Markings on the playground are of great help in organizing games, teaching subject matter, developing spatial skills, and teaching the names of simple geometric figures (see Chapters 6 and 8). The markings should be clearly drawn or painted on the playground, preferably on the blacktop area. If it is necessary to have markings overlap because of lack of space (see drawing, page 155), the overlapping markings can each be a different color. Dowels, rods, or ropes can be used instead of paint or chalk for many markings. They have the obvious advantage that they can be easily removed.

Indoor Space

For a class of thirty young children, the minimum area in the gymnasium should be about 2,400 square feet. A smaller area does not permit division of a class into groups to do different exercises simultaneously or to engage in creative movement.

Essentially the same equipment that is used on the playground can be used in the gym. Ropes and rings that must be fastened to special equipment outdoors can be hung from the ceiling if the room is built as a gymnasium.

Ideally, a separate room should be used for movement education with young children. We have at the Frostig Center a room measuring 40 feet by 31 feet, which is used for movement education for eight to ten children. The room contains no equipment and it is carpeted in a sunny yellow. We believe the carpeting and the brightness of the room help to stimulate the children to be creative. Apparatus is used only on the playground.

Small Equipment

Small equipment is of even greater importance than stationary apparatus. Most of the equipment can be used both indoors and outdoors. The following is a list of minimum supplies for use by kindergarten and primary school children in a well-balanced movement education program:

Balls. Nine-inch; one recommended for each child; at least one for two children.

Tennis balls. One recommended for every three children.

Beanbags. One recommended for each child; at least one for two children.

Wands, dowels, or rods. Twenty-four to 30 inches long and 1/2-inch in diameter; one recommended for each child; at least one for two children. These are used for going over and under, for stretching exercises, and for temporary markings on the floor.

Hoops* (wooden — plastic is too fragile). One recommended for each child; at least one for two children. Hoops are used for bowling with the hands or stick; for jumping and climbing through; as targets for balls and beanbags; as Hula Hoops; to teach children to work in small groups; and to develop movement sequences.

Ropes. One 10-foot; 6-foot jump ropes, one recommended for each child; at least one for two children.

Stretch rope.* At the Frostig Center, we have found a rubber stretch rope invaluable. The stretch rope is less dangerous than the usual rope because it is elastic and it gives if a child's foot or some

---

*One source for wooden hoops and stretch ropes is PESA, P.O. Box 292, Trumbull, Connecticut 06611.

other part of the body catches in it. If the two ends of the stretch rope are joined, the children may use it to learn to move in a circle. They gain immensely in body awareness and group awareness by performing various movements as a team. (See Chapter 12 for exercises.)

Cardboard discs. Ten 12-inch and 40 8-inch in diameter. These are used as stepping stones in balance exercises.

Mats. One for two children when no gym is available; two tumbling mats when a gym is available and the children can rest on the floor.

Tubes or tires. Three to 5.

Blocks. Ten to 15, 12-by 6-inch.

In addition, the teacher should have at least the following supplies:

Stopwatch.

Tape measure.

Record player and records.

Rhythm instruments, especially a tambourine.

Portable chalkboard.

Work Cited

Rasmus, C. J. A formula for play: Child + space + imagination. In *Physical Education for Children's Healthful Living.* Washington, D.C.: Bulletin No. 23-A, Association for Childhood Education International, 1968.

Chapter **11**

Structuring Movement Education

Although the central goals of movement education are unvarying, the emphasis of the program can be shifted to achieve particular purposes. Most frequently the teacher will emphasize the attributes of movement (balance and agility, for example) or focus on creative movement. But she should also give practice in translating sensory experiences into movement (following commands or copying a movement sequence) and in body awareness. The special needs of groups such as those with learning difficulties or the mentally retarded also have to be met.

The structure of each movement education session is influenced by all these considerations as well as by the physical environment, the maturity of the pupils, and the interests and training of the teacher. But above all, the structure of a session should be influenced by the children's reactions.

Flexibility of approach is important for all movement education (and indeed, for all teaching). A good teacher prepares a lesson plan, but she is prepared and willing to depart from it. The response of even one child may suggest that the lesson should be modified to serve the immediate detectable needs of all the children — to provide more or fewer strenuous exercises, to be more or less teacher-directed, or to proceed at a different pace. The teacher should also always consider the possibility of modifying an exercise for a particular child or letting the child modify it for himself.

Choice of Teaching Style

In teaching movement education, the teaching style — the "how" — is as important as the "what." The style of teaching should be chiefly aimed at making the children more self-reliant. Even young children can learn to become self-reliant, and the more self-directive they become, the fewer will be the discipline problems (Mosston, 1966). The amount of guidance the teacher gives depends upon the particular activity and the abilities of the children, but in general the teacher should give the minimum necessary to achieve the aims of any session or any activity within a session.

Youngsters must learn to be self-reliant if they are to become productive. We remember working with inner city children who huddled together for security, leaving no room for movement. Only after we had assuaged their anxiety did they dare stand so that each had sufficient space to move without interfering with another child. At a subsequent session, one of the youngsters shouted happily, "It's easy to find my place now. I just remember where I stood before. That's my place!" The same children were also unable to create movement sequences or vary any movement sequence independently. Although they quickly picked up new sequences and rules that were demonstrated or described in detail by the teacher, these children were unable to decide for themselves what to do. They equated independence of judgment, thought, and action with unruliness.

Children should be made aware, however, that independence does not mean loss of order and control. Most children become aware early in life that control of movement is essential if they are not to fall and to bump themselves, and eventually they can learn that such control is necessary for all their activities, as well as for maintaining their pleasure and spontaneity.

Inhibited children such as those described above can be helped if they first work in pairs. Although work in pairs usually follows individual work, the social relationship of helping and being helped makes the children feel more secure so that they can begin to be more independent. We have observed that even kindergarten children can learn to work as a group in an orderly, self-directed way, both in the classroom and on the playground. Creative movement is an excellent instrument for promoting self-direction. It provides children with the security that comes from experiencing relatedness to the group and to other individuals, and it teaches that joy can be derived from self-directed exploration (Chapter 5).

Competition

There should be little individual or group competition in movement education, especially with young children. Even later, competition should be avoided except in sports. Each youngster must learn to concentrate on his own performance as well as on cooperating with other children. In general, a child should compete only with himself in trying to improve his skills.

Incentives for Creative Movement

In Chapter 5, we described how the teacher encouraged a little girl
to create a dance in which she rocked her doll because she could
not let go of a scarf the way the other children could. The little
girl's dance suggested to the other children different movement sequences in which they showed how to carry things and how to care
for animals and people. The teacher encouraged the children to com-
pose movement sequences that suggested, for instance, carrying a
pitcher of water without spilling it, picking a flower and carrying it
to someone as a birthday gift, and restoring a young bird to its nest.
Then the teacher, in turn inspired by the children, told a story. She
explained to the children that they were to listen carefully so that
later they could act out the story.

"In a place in Brazil, dolphins live and play in a stream that runs
into a large river. One year there was very little rainfall, and the stream
did not have enough water to flow into the large river. The dolphins
were trapped in the stream. They could still play in the deep parts
of the stream, but they could not swim back to the large river. They
had to crowd together in the stream at the place where there was
the most water or they would die. They needed deeper water.

"A group of exploring scientists saw the dolphins and decided to
help them. They put a net across the stream, shouting and beating
the water with their paddles. The dolphins, frightened by the noise,
swam into the net. Then the scientists dragged the net to shore.
There were four dolphins in it.

"The scientists tied each of the dolphins to a board and carried
them all to the large river not far away. There they let the dolphins
go. The dolphins swam and played, happy to be back in deep water
again."

When the teacher had finished, she helped the children to evolve
a movement sequence based on the story. In it, the children did a
"dolphin swim," tumbled, rolled, jumped, and leaped. Then they
changed from free movements to more restricted movements to suggest the careful carrying of the dolphins; and then they went back
to free movements to suggest the dolphins' joy in being saved.

This anecdote illustrates how ideas and feelings can be used to
develop movement sequences. It also shows the beneficial interplay
that may develop between teacher and children if the teacher is flexible. A portion of a session can readily grow out of response to the
children's reactions.

Ideas much simpler than the dolphin story can be used, especially
with very young children. For example, they may be asked to walk

as if carrying a heavy package; or they may be told to imagine they have been given a new ball and asked to show how they throw it, catch it, bounce it, and dance around with it.

Using Music

Another important stimulus and accompaniment for movement is music. Whether music is melodic or percussive, children want to move and dance to it. Either a piano or records can be used to provide melody. A large selection of recordings especially made for children is available, and the teacher should choose the music best suited to the class.*

A percussion instrument, such as a tambourine, gong, cymbal, or bell, can be used to direct rhythm and quality (heavy-light).

With more advanced classes, a percussion instrument may be used to provide incentive for movement in the following way. The children walk in a circle while the teacher provides an unvarying, even beat with a tambourine or other instrument. If a child wants to break this somewhat irritating monotony, he moves into the middle of the circle to perform a movement sequence of his own creation. As soon as the child moves toward the center, the teacher stops the beat, and the other children stand still to watch. When the sequence is completed, the teacher resumes the beat, and the children continue to walk in a circle until another child wants to enter the free space and perform a movement sequence.

Movement can direct the percussion instrument, rather than vice versa, if a child establishes a rhythm by his movements. Another child or the teacher picks up the rhythm with the instrument. The rest of the children move to that rhythm. This procedure helps the children to become aware of the rhythm and movement of others, as well as their own.

It is important to remember that music should be used sparingly, however, for otherwise the children may be deprived of opportunities to create and follow their own rhythms.

Starting the Program

The teacher with a class that has not previously had this program — whether the children are kindergartners or third graders — should

---

*The following albums from the *Discovering Music Together Series* are available from Follett Educational Corporation: L001; L100; L100R; L200; L200R; L300; L400. *Discovering Music Together — Early Childhood* is a teacher's edition. It emphasizes creative movement.

begin with informal introductory sessions. These introductory sessions should be structured to provide information concerning the children's responses to various aspects of movement education. The teacher cannot construct lessons for her class without knowing in what areas the children may need special help.

Following are the points that the teacher should observe during introductory sessions:

1. Mechanics: Are the children able to proceed in an orderly fashion to the area set aside for movement education (playground, gymnasium, homeroom area)? Are they able to get needed equipment, such as balls or hoops, upon request? Can they make any necessary adaptations in clothing, such as removing and putting on shoes and stockings and outdoor clothing? Can they line up and form a circle, for instance?

2. Locomotor skills: Can the children run, gallop, skip?

3. Body position: Can the children assume simple positions upon request, such as crouching or sitting with crossed legs?

4. Vocabulary: Do the children understand simple terms? For instance, a child may be able to execute a movement such as a gallop when he can watch others but not be able to initiate it because he has never heard the word *gallop.*

5. Relational and comparative terms: Words such as *in, beside, faster, wider* may be confusing to some children. Also, some children may not know the names of parts of the body, such as *knee, elbow, shoulders.* (See Chapter 6.)

6. Understanding directions: Can the children execute simple directions upon request, such as "Walk to the door" or "Clap your hands." (See also Chapter 6.)

7. Memory: How well does each child remember a movement or movement sequence practiced previously? Does a child remember his initial position in the room after moving away from it? Can he remember a sequence of instructions? (See also Chapter 6.)

8. Use of space: Each child needs to explore the space he shares with others — the common space; and the space he needs to move while in one spot — the personal space. How proficient are the children in relating a point of the body to certain spaces? For example, can a child respond correctly to "Put your hand in the triangle. Put your head and shoulders inside the hoop"?

9. Using equipment: Do the children know at least one use for each piece of equipment? Do they know the names? Do they know the safety rules for each (if necessary)? Does one child react strongly to a piece of equipment (either very negatively or very positively)?

10. Individual reactions: Are certain children hyperactive? Hypo-

active? Do some respond very strongly to the teacher? To other children? Do some children react positively or negatively to music (an important consideration for children with learning difficulties)?

11. Interaction among the children: Can the children use the common space without endangering other children? Can a child relate his body to another child upon request, such as "Stand in front of your partner" or "Stand behind him"?

The activities chosen for these introductory sessions should be simple. The children may run, skip, clap to music, join hands with a partner, step over a stick, throw and catch a beanbag, and use playground equipment while the teacher observes carefully.

The teacher need have no fear that children who are skilled in some or most of the attributes of movement will be bored with the simpler activities. Children who love to skip when they are three years old still love to skip when they are ten — and even into adulthood!

The informal, introductory phase will vary considerably in length for different groups of children, even between different classes at the same grade level in the same public school. It may last for one session for some groups, a few weeks for others, and months for some brain-damaged children. Even for the latter group the variations may be great.

The point at which the teacher moves on to more difficult activities depends not only on the movement skills of the children but even more on how well the class members cooperate with each other and how they respond to the creative movement elements of the program.

The Exercises and "Programming"

It is not possible to minutely and rigorously "program" movement education. In contrast to teaching the sciences, teaching the arts should not proceed in a linear fashion. The arts present a comprehensive temporal-spatial patterning rather than a hierarchical sequencing of skills.

This program is not designed to teach only skills, although that is a very important part of it. It is designed to help children express themselves through movement, to become more aware of themselves and others, and to become more aware of feelings and how feelings are aroused by movement. Any sequence of movements involves different attributes in which different children may be proficient to different degrees. One child may be advanced in a particular activity or in some aspect of the activity and another child may be backward in the same activity. Different variations of the same exercise may therefore have to be used with the two children.

Since exercises involving endurance, competitive games, and acrobatic stunts are more suitable for children beyond the third or fourth grade, they have been minimized in this program. Below that level, step-by-step programming is possible and necessary when specific attributes of movement are the main focus: for example, it is possible for a child to become more flexible through training. But here again, the abilities of children in one class may differ so much that it is impossible to set a standard for the classroom as a whole. The growth of children's physical skills is not determined by their overall rate of growth. Chronological age does not by itself define physical skill or the ability to express oneself through movement.

In the exercises there is no strict progression from the simplest to the most difficult. Some exercises at or near the end of a section may be easier than some of those given earlier. Coordination Exercises 16-19, for instance, are beanbag throwing and catching, but they are simpler than some coordination exercises with lower numbers. This is simply because exercises requiring equipment have been put at or near the end of each section. Beanbag (and ball) catching should be introduced to children very early in the program, as should other simple exercises requiring equipment.

The variations within an exercise do for the most part progress from easiest to most difficult for most children. Exceptions occur when an easy variation must be interpolated in order to progress smoothly to a more complex variation.

Lesson Plan Guidelines

Although flexibility must be maintained in planning a movement education session, the lessons should be carefully planned and the teaching principles should be consistent. Following are important guidelines that will enable the teacher to construct useful lesson plans based on the principles of the program.

1. The teacher is reminded that the children should have some form of movement education on every school day.

2. The mechanics of the movement education session must be taught — where to line up, where to stand during exercises on the spot, how to get and return equipment, for instance.

3. If some children do not know the basic forms of locomotion, such as skipping, hopping, jumping, and running, they should be taught and given many chances to practice.

4. Every session should begin with a warm-up exercise — one that

requires vigorous activity to ensure that blood circulation and breathing are speeded up and that the children are both mentally alert and physically prepared for the lesson.

5. The activities in each session should be arranged so that a relatively vigorous activity is followed by a relaxing one.

6. The teacher should not emphasize one aspect of the program at the expense of another, for example, creative movement to the exclusion of work on the attributes of movement.

7. Two or three new exercises should be added at each session, and exercises introduced previously should be reviewed or repeated.

8. The teacher should not attempt to have the children do all the variations of an exercise during one session. Many of the variations are quite difficult, and very young children or children with learning difficulties may not be able to do them.

9. Exercises on the spot and exercises involving locomotion should be included in each session.

10. Body positions should be varied in on-the-spot exercises (lying on the floor, crouching, standing, for example) as well as during locomotion.

11. Lengthy exercises, such as those to help children learn a movement sequence, recognize shapes, or follow written commands, need not be included in every session. They should be used only when it is desirable to integrate such specific objectives with the curriculum for a specific child, group, or class.

12. When constructing a lesson, the teacher should note that many of the exercises train more than one attribute of movement. If she wishes the children to work on agility, for example, she should not be restricted to looking only in the agility section of Chapter 12 for suitable exercises.

13. The exercises should involve several attributes of movement. The groups of exercises discussed on pages 186 to 188, for example, include rope jumping, which strengthens the leg muscles and develops agility, coordination, and balance; crossing a room in different movement patterns, which develops agility and coordination; and throwing a beanbag, which develops whole-body coordination as well as eye-hand coordination. In succeeding sessions, the teacher should include exercises for other attributes of movement, such as trying to touch the floor with the fingers by bending forward with legs straight, which develops flexibility. It is also advantageous to include an exercise requiring a different body position, such as sitting or lying down. Speed may also be emphasized.

14. With all children, but particularly with the physically handicapped, the teacher must notice immediately when a child needs as-

sistance. Assistance may take several forms, including anchoring a body part (see example, pages 51 and 52), having a child do the exercise sitting rather than standing, or by actively giving other help. Sometimes a child may be able to perform a movement successfully after the relevant body part is carefully touched (for instance, the knee when the child is asked to raise his knee). Sometimes more active help has to be given, and the teacher may move together with the child or support his body.

15. Each child should exercise alone, with a partner, and in a group. Exercises in which children coordinate their movements or give each other support have a therapeutic effect, including making a child feel more secure, more accepted, more able to control himself, and better able to adjust to others. For these reasons, such exercises should be included in the program as soon as possible (although they may be too difficult at the start, especially for handicapped children). As the children develop skills, more work with partners and groups should be included, and some such work should be a part of every movement education session.

16. Some work with equipment and music may be included in each lesson, but a large part of a session should be done without either so that the children can concentrate on their own bodies and rhythms.

17. The teacher should be continually aware that a great variety of abilities — memory, concentration, associative processes, for example — can be enhanced through movement.

18. The sessions should be enjoyable. The children should feel after each session that they have had a good time and done a laudable job.

Developing Movement Skills

Although the exercises in this chapter are grouped according to the emphasis on a specific attribute of movement, no exercise trains only one attribute, and many give equal emphasis to more than one. Moreover, certain basic forms of locomotion, such as galloping, hopping, skipping, leaping, whirling, jumping, rolling, crawling, scooting, walking on all fours, walking in a crouch position, or a combination of these, can be adapted to involve any movement attribute.

A change in the directions can change the emphasis of an exercise from one attribute to another. If the basic movement is running, for example, the exercise emphasizes speed if the teacher asks the children to run back and forth only once but as fast as they can. If, when the children are running she adds, "When I say 'Stop!' you are to stop at once and stand very still," she changes the emphasis to balance and coordination. If there are obstacles in the running area necessitating frequent changes of direction, the main emphasis is on agility and body awareness.

The emphasis on an attribute of movement thus depends on the specific form or combination in which an exercise is presented. The teacher should be aware that quite minor changes in the directions to the children can alter completely the effect of these exercises.

There are also many exercises, such as those for strengthening specific muscle groups and for developing static balance, flexibility, fine muscle coordination, and body awareness, that do not involve locomotion but only a change of body position or the movement of specific body parts. Such exercises are intrinsically more appropriate for a single specific attribute of movement. They can be adapted much less readily for more than one purpose.

When it is possible to adapt exercises, it is important to use the opportunity for promoting the children's imaginations. Even where the instructions give variations, the teacher should ask the children for their own suggestions and let them try them out. This gives children a much greater sense of participation, besides promoting creativity and expressive language. Many of the agility exercises can be performed in a variety of body positions, which the children may initiate. When, for example, performing Agility Exercise 3 (Treasures from Across the Sea) a child may carry the beanbag on his back while crawling, on his head while walking, in his lap while scooting, and in many other ways with different body positions.

Variations are suggested for many of the exercises (the skipping exercises, for example), and the variations are usually presented in the order of difficulty. As a rule, not more than two variations should be attempted in any session except when children invent their own variations.

A different type of adaptation may have to be practiced if no large space is available for movement education. Most of the exercises can be performed in the classroom provided the space is used economically and the exercises requiring expansive movements are adjusted to it. Some exercises can, for example, be done while the children are seated at or on their desks, instead of on the floor. And some group games can be undertaken if the class is divided into groups that do different activities simultaneously — some children at their desks or in the aisles while others use the larger space at the front of the room.

The instructions rarely include recommendations for the length of time or number of repetitions for an exercise. These depend upon the age, stamina, and capabilities of the children in a class. The time must therefore be determined by the teacher. She should keep in mind that although each exercise should fulfill its purpose, it should not be at the risk of either straining the children or letting them lose interest. It is usually better to use the same exercise a number of times, each time for a relatively brief period, than to use it once or twice for extended periods.

The exercises should also be considered examples that the teacher may use as a basis to create other exercises, although the inexperienced teacher will need to follow the directions closely. The experienced teacher, however, may develop many other similar exercises and help the children develop still others.

Finally, a suggestion with regard to exercises in which the children perform animal walks: Before performing such an exercise for the first time, the children should at least be shown pictures of the animal, and if possible movies or filmstrips in which the animal is seen in motion. Of greatest value is a trip to a zoo for the specific purpose of studying the various animal movements.

Coordination and Rhythm

Both coordination and rhythm are characteristics of every movement. Rhythm depends upon coordination, and thus it is an integral part of training in coordination.

Basic movements requiring coordination and rhythm, such as skipping, galloping, and simple folk dance steps, should be practiced frequently, both with and without music.

The exercises should be done in pairs and small groups, as well as singly. For example, the children should skip while holding hands, either in the usual way or with their arms crossed in front. Side steps may be performed while holding hands face to face or back to back.

Training in rhythm involves conscious synchronization of movement through either an inner natural and individual rhythm or through rhythm provided by music.

Rhythmic exercises in which each child follows his own inner rhythm are important in the development of body awareness and have been discussed in Chapter 4.

If exercises are done to music, an external rhythm is imposed. Care must be taken, however, not to use music so extensively that it hinders the development of inner rhythm. Nevertheless, some training with music helps the development of children's inner rhythm and coordination and constitutes one of the most joyous of activities.

Coordination — 1 (Crossing the Midline)

Collecting Seashells

1. The children walk forward, going into a knee bend with every step (half-squatting position). They pick up an imaginary seashell with the hand opposite to the forward foot. The shell lies just ahead of the foot. The children should advance with a steady rhythmic swing, without pausing after picking up each shell.

The teacher might say, "Now let's pretend that we are going to walk on the beach and collect seashells. To pick them up you have to bend close to the ground like this (demonstrate). When *this* foot comes forward (indicate left), you pick up a shell on the sand in front of it with *this* hand (indicate right). When *this* foot comes forward (indicate right), pick up a shell in front of it with *this* hand (indicate left). Use the hand on the opposite side of the foot that is in front. Watch while I do it. Here's another shell! Right foot, left hand. All right, now you try."

2. Similar movement, but the children pick up the seashell with the hand on the same side as the forward foot.

3. The children pretend to be skipping along the beach. At a signal (a handclap or beat of a tambourine), they pretend to see a shell and bend to pick it up; then they continue skipping. The movement should be as smooth and flowing as possible.

4. As 3, but without a signal. Each child runs, skips, or walks his own course, bending to pick up shells in his own rhythm.

Coordination – 2

Troll's Walk

1. The children pretend to be trolls. They walk, raising their knees and stamping their feet. Their trunks are bent forward because they are angry. Their arms are stiff and their fists are clenched.

2. The trolls begin to feel less angry. Although they are still bent forward, their arms swing easily as they walk. They do not stamp so hard.

3. The trolls are no longer angry. They raise their feet high over roots and stones, but their bodies are now straight. They feel strong, proud, and happy.

The teacher may say, "Today we are going to do the Troll's Walk. Does anyone know what a troll is? That's right. It's an imaginary creature. Some people imagine that a troll is a sort of elf with an eye in the middle of his forehead, who lives in the caves or hills hidden in the forests of countries called Norway, Sweden, and Denmark. (Show pictures if possible.) Trolls are supposed to be ill-tempered, and often they are angry, but sometimes they are happy.

"First, can you imitate a troll who is angry? He walks like this. He lifts his knees up so that he won't trip over roots and stones. And when he is angry he humps his back, keeps his arms straight and very stiff, clenches his fists, and stamps his feet down at each step. Now can you do it? Remember, you are very angry. Maybe some forest animal has taken your dinner! Good.

"Now you have found some berries to eat, so you aren't as angry. Can you keep walking the same way, but not stamp? Can you let your arms swing forward as they normally do? Good. Now you have found some honey and a lot of good things to eat. You don't feel angry anymore. You are strong and proud and happy. Can you keep your legs and arms moving the same way, but straighten your backs and stand up tall? Fine. You are a wonderful group of trolls."

The teacher may then play In the Hall of the Mountain King from Grieg's Peer Gynt, Suite 1, and have the children move to the music.

Coordination – 3 (Crossing the Midline)
FLEXIBILITY (Shoulder, hip joints; spine)
BALANCE (Static, dynamic)

Pulleys

The teacher should explain what a pulley is and demonstrate with pictures and objects.

1. The children lie on the floor faceup. They raise each leg alternately to a vertical position, keeping the legs straight.

2. The children raise each arm alternately, keeping the legs flat on the floor.

3. The children raise both legs together, lower them, and then raise the left arm and the left leg together. Lower; repeat with right arm and right leg. Continue.

4. The children raise the right arm and the left leg; then the left arm and the right leg.

5. As 4, but in the standing position, raising the legs alternately to a horizontal position and touching them with the opposite hand. Those who are able to do so should move the shoulder and hip joints only, keeping the trunk as still and upright as possible. Children who have difficulty with balance may stand with their backs against a wall for support or another child may steady them by holding a hand.

6. The children stand with feet apart. They bend forward and touch the opposite foot (requires trunk movement and considerable flexibility).

7. As 5, but the children step forward, swinging the free leg up with each step and touching the foot with the opposite hand.

8. As 7, but the children step backward and touch the foot with the opposite hand.

Coordination – 4

Side Step and Slide Step

1. The children walk sideways, placing one foot to the side and then placing the other beside it. After moving in one direction in this way, they should move in the other.

2. As 1, but the children slide their feet along the floor.

3. The children slide two steps forward, leading with the left foot and sliding the right foot up to it; then two steps to the side, leading with the right foot and bringing the left foot up to it; then two steps backward, leading with the right foot; then two steps to the left so that the children describe a square. The movement should be repeated, leading with the right foot and going sideways to the left.

4. The children pretend they are ice-skating and move freely in any direction. One foot should lead for a time, then the other foot. The movement should be as flowing and rhythmic as possible.

Coordination – 5

BALANCE (Dynamic)

Tightrope Walk

1. The children step forward with the right foot; then they move the left foot forward, placing the left heel in front of the right toes

and against them. Then they place the right heel against the left toes. Repeat, beginning with the other foot.

2. The children step forward with the right foot, bring the left foot up to it, placing the toes behind the right heel. They again move the right foot forward and follow it with the left foot. Repeat, beginning with the other foot.

3. Accelerate the tempo.

4. The children experiment with Variations 1 and 2 in any combination they want. They demonstrate their sequences to each other.

5. The children perform the variations in pairs, proceeding side by side, their arms crossed in front and holding hands.

Coordination — 6 (Crossing the midline)
Cross-Over Walk

1. The children walk sideways in a straight line, placing the left foot to the side and crossing the right foot in front of it. They return in the other direction, crossing the left foot in front of the right.

2. As 1, but crossing one foot behind the other.

3. The children cross in front and back alternately. They should remain facing the teacher without turning the trunk.

4. As 3, but in pairs, the children facing each other and holding hands.

Coordination — 7
Bear Walk

1. The children walk on their hands and feet, keeping their legs and arms straight. The arm and leg on the same side move together.

2. As 1, but the children's elbows and knees are bent.

3. As 1, but the children keep one foot off the floor. (The bear is lame.)

4. The children are told to think of other animals to imitate. They may suggest a dog (Coordination Exercise 9); a crab (Coordination Exercise 11); a rabbit (Coordination Exercise 14); a duck (Agility Exercise 14); a kangaroo (Agility Exercise 18); a seal (Strength Exercise 15); an inchworm (Strength Exercise 16); an elephant (Flexibility Exercise 6); or a giraffe (Balance Exercise 9).

They may imitate one of the animals during this period or during a future period. They should guess which animal each child imitates.

Coordination — 8 (Crossing the midline)
Crawling (Cross-lateral)

The teacher should demonstrate 1 and 2, step by step. The children should not crawl for longer than they enjoy the exercise because it is hard on the knees.

1. The children begin on their hands and knees, hands below shoulders, knees under hips. They move one arm and the opposite leg forward at the same time. The head should be turned toward the shoulder of the arm that is not extended. Continue with the opposite arm and leg.

2. The children crawl backward after mastering 1.

3. The children crawl in a variety of patterns and directions. They may inscribe circles and other geometric figures or change direction as freely as they want.

4. The children make U-turns at walls or lines without breaking the rhythm or sequence of movements.

5. The children name the parts of their bodies as they move them (right hand, left leg, left leg, right hand, etc.).

Coordination — 9

Dog Walk and Run

1. The children walk and then run on all fours. Their knees should be slightly bent. The opposite arm and leg move together.

2. The children pretend to be lame dogs. They walk on only one foot and two hands, trailing the lame leg behind. They can then try to run in this manner.

3. As 2, but the children walk on two feet and one hand.

Coordination — 10

Blindfolded Crawling

The purpose of blindfolding is to eliminate visual cues, thus emphasizing kinesthetic and tactile cues. It also helps to establish firm right-left differentiation independent of visual cues.

1. The teacher blindfolds the children and puts a weighted band on one arm of each child (the arm of the dominant hand) to identify one side of the body as the "heavy" side. The children move forward with regular cross-pattern crawling according to directions, such as "Right arm, left leg; left arm, right leg." The children practice until they can move rhythmically following the directions.

2. Still wearing blindfolds and weighted bands, the children practice both cross-pattern and one-sided crawling (arm and leg on the same side move at the same time). The teacher alternates the types of crawling.

Coordination — 11
AGILITY
Crab Walk

The children squat. They reach backward and place their hands flat on the floor behind their hips without sitting down. They raise the pelvis as high as possible and move first backward and then forward in this position, keeping the head, neck, and trunk parallel to the floor.

Coordination — 12
BALANCE (Dynamic)
STRENGTH (Shoulder girdle, trunk muscles, buttocks)

The Tunnel

1. The children sit on the floor, knees pulled close to the body, feet flat. They lean backward, placing their hands behind them and to the sides on the floor. They raise themselves on hands and feet, pushing the trunk upward until roughly parallel to the floor, and then return to the sitting position.

The next variation may be too difficult for most children below third-grade level.

2. When in the raised position, the children are told to turn over so that they face the floor. They must not touch the floor with any part of the body except the hands and feet. Each child attempts to solve this problem for himself. Those who do it successfully demonstrate to the others. They should try to keep the trunk horizontal while turning.

Coordination — 13
STRENGTH (Leg muscles)
SPEED
AGILITY

Magpie, Magpie, Hop Quickly to Your Nest

The teacher should explain what a magpie is and show pictures of one.

1. The children practice a bird hop. With feet together, they go forward in little hops.

2. The children hop forward as fast as possible. They may race.

3. The children hop forward, holding a beanbag between their knees.

4. Enough beanbags for all of the magpies are put in the middle of the room. Each magpie runs to a beanbag, takes it between his feet without using his hands, and hops quickly back to his nest with it.

5. The game can be played with one beanbag fewer than the number of children. The magpie who fails to get a beanbag must collect all of the beanbags and return them to the middle of the room so that the game can be played again. If there are more than eight children, there should be fewer beanbags so that two or more children get no beanbags and share in collecting them.

Coordination — 14
AGILITY
STRENGTH (Leg muscles)

Rabbit Hop
1. The children crouch, hands touching the floor between their feet. They jump forward, landing in the same position, and continue in a straight line across the room.
2. The children pretend they are young rabbits who are happy because they have been allowed to go out and play in an open field. They can hop and tumble in any direction.

Coordination — 15
AGILITY

Galloping
1. The children gallop in a circle as if they are circus horses.
2. The children change direction at the beat of a percussion instrument.
3. The children move individually, changing from galloping to trotting, running, or walking, as they want.
4. The children demonstrate their movement sequences to each other.

The teacher may have the children perform any of the steps in pairs, holding hands normally or with arms crossed behind their backs.

If a child has difficulty in galloping, he may practice by lying on his back and making a bicycling movement with his legs in a one-two, one-two rhythm. If necessary, the teacher guides his legs. The teacher should show the child that the motion of pulling his knees toward his body alternatingly is the same as in galloping, although the rhythm is more even.

Coordination — 16
AGILITY

Bump Your Knee and Touch Your Heel (Skipping)
1. The children skip around the room.
2. As 1, but at every skip the children bump the knee of the skip-

ping leg with the other knee, letting the lower part of the free leg swing out to the side.

3. While skipping, the children reach backward and touch the foot of the raised leg with the hand on the same side.

4. The children invent their own variations of the skipping exercise. They should try to include turns in their movement patterns.

Catching and Throwing Games

Beanbag and ball games provide excellent training in eye-hand coordination; kicking games in eye-foot coordination. Little agility is involved when an object is thrown or caught in a standing position. To incorporate agility, movements such as running and jumping should be included as the beanbag or ball is caught or avoided.

Throwing and catching ball games can also be played with beanbags. Since beanbags are easier to handle, they should be used first.

The beanbag and ball games described are examples, given in order of difficulty. Teachers know or can devise many more.

Throwing and catching beanbags is one of the first steps in learning eye-hand coordination.

Coordination – 17

Catching Beanbags Individually (Stationary)

1. Each child throws a beanbag into the air and catches it.
2. The children throw beanbags into the air and clap their hands before catching.
3. The children throw beanbags into the air and jump before catching.
4. As 3, but the children land with one leg in front, the other behind. They switch the position of the legs with each jump.

Coordination – 18

Catching Beanbags Individually (In motion)

1. The children walk while throwing beanbags in the air and catching them.
2. As 1, but the children run.
3. As 2, but the children change direction while running.

Coordination – 19

Catching Beanbags with a Partner

1. Two children stand about five feet apart and throw a beanbag to each other.
2. The distance between the partners is gradually increased until the children cannot catch the beanbag easily.

Coordination – 20

Throwing Beanbags at a Target

The teacher draws squares on the playground with chalk or puts out hoops or empty boxes to throw into.

1. The children stand in pairs quite close to the squares or boxes and try to throw beanbags into them.
2. The throwing distance is increased as the children become more skillful.
3. The children are told to walk to a goal and that they must throw a beanbag into each of a number of targets along the way. They retrieve the beanbag after each throw and proceed with it to the next target. The target areas may be drawn on the playground or marked by sticks, hoops, or ropes.

Organized Ball Play

Before organized ball play is introduced, the children should be given opportunities to experiment freely by bouncing, catching, and throwing balls – individually, with a partner, and against a wall.

Exercises then can be introduced involving simple catching, letting the ball bounce before catching it, and performing jumps or hand-claps before catching it, as with beanbags.

Coordination — 21

Spokes in a Wheel
The children sit on the floor in circles of 8- to 10-feet in diameter, six children to a circle. Their legs are straight and apart. One child sits in the center.

1. The child in the center rolls or bounces a ball to a child in the circle. That child rolls or bounces it back to the center child, who continues with the next child in the circle. When every child has returned the ball to the center, all the wheel spokes have been put in. Another child then becomes the "hub."

2. When the children can perform the exercise proficiently, the pace should be increased.

Coordination — 22

Bowling
The children, in groups of two or three, roll a ball at plastic bowling pins or milk cartons. After each child bowls, he goes behind the pins and sets up those knocked over by the next bowler.

Coordination — 23

Back and Forth
This ball game helps children to learn to gauge distance.

The children stand in two lines about six feet apart, each child facing a partner. Behind each child in one line are three markers, each one a yard behind the other.

Each child in one line throws a ball to his partner in the other line. The receiver returns it.

When both children have caught the ball three times, one child steps back to the first marker behind him, and the throwing and catching is resumed. When each has caught the ball three times, another yard is added to the distance. After the third marker is reached, the distance is decreased in the same way.

Coordination — 24

Bouncing in the Hoop
A hoop or tire is placed on the ground. Two children stand on either side of it a short distance away. One child tries to throw a ball into the hoop. His partner catches the ball after it bounces and returns it the same way.

The children should stand close enough to the target to ensure success, but the distance should be gradually increased by the teacher, according to the abilities of the children.

Coordination – 25

Hot Potato

The children stand in a circle, and every third child is given a tennis ball. Each ball represents a hot potato, which, if it is held too long, "burns." Each child with a ball throws it immediately to any other child whose hands are empty.

Any child who drops a ball or throws it erratically must take the ball (now a cold potato) to the oven to warm it up. The oven is a designated area in which the child throws the ball up and catches it ten times before rejoining the group.

Coordination – 26

Round the World

1. The children stand in circles (up to ten children in each) and pass a ball quickly from one to the other around the circle. If a child drops the ball, everyone shouts, "Get it!" He must retrieve the ball and run around the circle with it, handing it on when he returns to his place. When the teacher or a leader shouts, "Round the World!" any child holding the ball must run around the circle with it.

2. As 1, but the children stand farther apart so that they must throw the ball to each other.

If the children know songs that they can sing to accompany the game, their enjoyment will be greater.

Coordination – 27

AGILITY

Figure Jumping

The teacher forms shapes, such as squares, triangles, and rectangles, on the floor with rods.

Each child in turn is asked to stand next to a shape and then jump into it with both feet together. If the children have previously learned the names of the shapes, they should call them out as they jump.

Coordination – 28

Walk the Dots

The teacher puts sixteen medium size discs on the floor in four rows of four discs each.

Each child is given a card on which a plan of the discs is drawn and a route is marked. Each child jumps from disc to disc following the route marked on his card. A card might, for example, be marked in the following way:

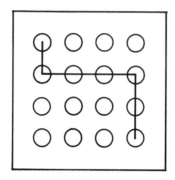

Coordination — 29
AGILITY
STRENGTH (Leg muscles)

Basic Rope Jumping

1. The children jump forward and if able to do so, also backward over a rope lying on the ground, first with both feet at once; then they start on both feet and land on one foot.

2. As 1, but the rope is held by two other children a few inches from the ground.

3. The children are told to go over or under the rope in any way they want.

4. The children jump over a rope that is swung slowly back and forth. They should try to maintain a steady rhythm.

5. Each child jumps over a short rope, which he turns himself.

6. Each child jumps over a long rope turned by two other children.

Coordination — 30
AGILITY
STRENGTH (Leg muscles)

Advanced Rope Jumping

When the children can jump rope gracefully and with clearly defined jumps, they may undertake more complex steps.

1. One child at a time stands close to the rope, and when it is turned jumps from side to side. (The child jumping faces one of the children turning the rope.)

2. Same as 1, but the children jump on one foot.

3. Same as 1, but the children make a quarter-turn in the air while jumping.

4. One child at a time runs to the rope and jumps it as it is turned (either toward or away from the jumper).

5. As 4, but the children make a half-turn while jumping.

6. The children use individual ropes and cross the arms in front.

7. As 6, but the children omit the intermediate steps between jumps.

8. As 6, but the children jump with feet apart and together alternately.

9. Same as 1, but the children pull the knees up to the chest while jumping.

10. Same as 1, but the children kick the legs out like scissors while jumping.

11. Same as 1, but the children make a bicycling movement while jumping.

Children should be encouraged to use any other steps they know. They often know chants to accompany the jumping.

Stretch Rope and Trampoline Board

Stretch-rope and trampoline-board exercises should be worked out by the children with the teacher's assistance. Children usually choose to start with simple movements and gradually develop more complex movements and sequences. If they do not, the teacher should guide them. The teacher may also have to regulate the pace of development, but she should be careful not to inhibit creativity or to impose too strongly her own ideas.

The following are exercises developed by children at the Frostig Center. They are given to show the diversity of movements and sequences that the equipment can stimulate. They should not be used as formal exercises.

Coordination — 31

AGILITY

Stretch Rope

1. The ends of the stretch rope are tied together to form a circle. The children stand in a circle, all facing in one direction, each child holding the rope lightly with the inside hand. They run in a circle, continuing to hold the rope.

2. The children stand inside the rope circle, holding the rope at waist level by gentle pressure with their bodies. They run in a circle, continuing to support the rope with their bodies.

3. As 2, but at a signal the children reverse the direction by stop-

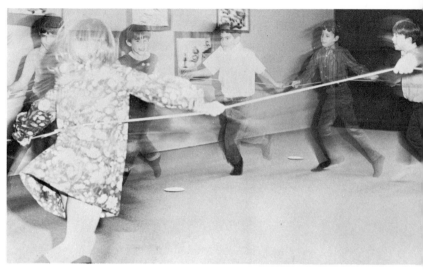

Running in a circle with a stretch rope is quite an art.

ping and turning. They then walk in the opposite direction, still sustaining the rope by body pressure.

4. As 3, but the children may use any movement or combination of movements as they circle, such as skipping, hopping, or jumping.

5. As 3, but when the children turn at the signal, they drop to their knees for a few seconds, rise, turn, and proceed without letting the rope fall.

6. The children make geometric shapes with the rope, standing inside the rope and forming corners with their bodies. (They decide who should stand where to produce a shape.)

7. The children experiment with forming shapes such as stars by designating certain children to move away from the circle at a signal, pulling the rope with them to form the shape.

8. Two children stand opposite each other, feet astride, and pull the rope in two parallel lines with their ankles, a few inches from the ground. The other children take turns in performing a sequence of steps along the length of it, first jumping over one strand and then over the other in any pattern they want. As they do so, they may turn, go sideways or backward, crouch, jump high, hop on one foot, or perform any other movement.

9. As 8, but the children jump forward or sideways over both strands at one time or over each strand in succession.

10. Two children stretch the rope in two strands — one low and one high — to constitute an obstacle course. The children crawl under the low strand and step over the high one.

Coordination — 32
AGILITY
BALANCE (Dynamic)
Trampoline Board

1. The children make small jumps with feet together.

2. As 1, but the children alternately kick right and left feet forward with heels on the board.

3. As 1, but the children kick with the right foot forward on alternating jumps.

4. As 1, but the children kick with feet together and apart alternately.

5. As 1, but the children interpolate large jumps at regular intervals.

6. The children make large jumps, drawing the knees up as high as possible.

7. As 6, but the children interpolate "star jumps" (large jumps with legs and arms flung wide to form an X) at regular intervals.

Trampoline boards stimulate children to jump in an endless variety of styles and patterns.

8. The children repeat any of the above steps but while turning in any way they want.

9. As 8, but the children make quarter-, half-, or full-turns in the air as directed.

10. The children do different steps and jumps on one foot with or without turning.

11. The children do steps and jumps with eyes closed.

12. The children jump, do a half-turn or full-turn and land with feet on the ground straddling the board; they jump back onto the board and repeat.

13. The children do small jumps, landing at regular intervals on the ground with feet straddling the board.

14. The children combine steps and jumps in any sequence.

15. As 14, but the children jump in any rhythm.

16. As 14, but the children use a jump rope.

17. As 14, but the children jump with one foot on the board, one off.

18. The children make a designated number of small jumps (six, for example); then land with feet straddling the board; then one jump less than the first time; then land straddling; and so on, one jump less each time.

19. If several boards are available, the children jump from one board to another.

20. Two or more children coordinate their movements. For example, one child may start from the right side of the board, jump onto it twice, and then jump off the left side. Another child then starts from the left side, jumps onto the board twice, and then jumps off the right side. A third child starts from the right side, and so on.

Agility

Agility is a prime factor when the body position is changed with skill and precision because it helps to maintain balance and to continue a redirected movement. It is needed in using climbing apparatus, in obstacle runs, in tumbling, and later in such sports as skiing, climbing, and pole vaulting.

Agility – 1
SPEED

The Big Giant (Tag game)
One child, the Big Giant, lives in the "meadow" in the center of the playground. On one side of the playground are the other chil-

dren, who want to cross the meadow to the "forest" on the other side.

The giant shouts, "Who's afraid of the big strong giant?" The children answer, "No one!" and try to run across the meadow to the forest without being caught by the giant, who is not allowed to leave the meadow. Whoever is caught is the giant next time.

Agility — 2
SPEED

Contest of the Seasons

The children stand along two chalklines about 20 feet apart, facing each other. No more than six children should be on each team. The leader of each team adopts the name of a season, and the other children on his team are each given a name appropriate to the season. Summer, for example, may have Flower, Bee, Sun, Beach, and Ice Cream on his team; Winter may have Frost, Icicle, Hibernating Bear, Skiis, and Christmas on his. The children try to remember as many names as possible.

Winter asks Summer for one of his subjects. If he remembers a name correctly (Bee, for example), all of the children run to the opposite chalkline while Winter tries to tag as many of Summer's team as he can before they reach the opposite line. Those he tags must go into the storehouse. Summer then asks Winter for one of his subjects, and the same change of teams occurs. The first leader to tag three children is the victor. If either calls a wrong name or cannot remember a name, all of the children in the storehouse are released and the game begins anew. The children then say their names to help Winter and Summer remember them.

The organization of this game takes considerable time. The game should be planned when the teacher wants an interval of rest for the children after strenuous exercise.

Agility — 3
COORDINATION

Treasures from Across the Sea

The children are sailors, each with a bag of treasures (beanbag) to bring home. They must cross a beach where pirates live, and therefore they must keep their hands free to defend themselves.

Each child should find his own solution. For example, one child might carry the treasure on his shoulder; another between his ankles; another on the back of his neck as he walks with head bent; and still another on his back while crawling. Or a child may kick the treasure across the beach; another may slide with his foot; still another may push it with his nose.

As in all exercises in which the class finds various solutions, the children should observe and learn from each other's solutions.

Agility — 4
STRENGTH (Leg muscles)

Jumping the Beanbag

1. Each child throws a beanbag on the ground about two feet ahead of himself, jumps over it, picks up the beanbag, throws it down, jumps over it again, and so on until he reaches a predetermined goal.

2. Sometimes a child should throw the beanbag slightly to the right or to the left so that he must make a turn in the air to jump over it.

3. The children vary their jumps according to their own ideas. For example, they may raise the knees high; keep the knees straight and legs together; bump the knee and touch the heel (Coordination Exercise 16); jump from a crouch position; or leap with one leg stretched forward, one back.

4. Use 1 as a relay race.

Agility — 5

Cuckoo in the Nest

Before playing the game, the teacher explains that cuckoos lay their eggs in the nests of other birds, and she gives other information about cuckoos. She may also sing or teach the children a song about cuckoos.

One child is the cuckoo. The other children are divided into groups of three. Two children in each trio face each other and hold hands. The third child stands between them "in the nest." The cuckoo does not have a nest. At a signal from the teacher, the children in the nests "fly" out and run around with the cuckoo. When the cuckoo cries "Cuckoo," all of the birds, including the cuckoo, try to get into new nests. The child who is left over becomes the new cuckoo.

Agility — 6

Follow the Leader

This game may be varied in many ways. Following are four versions.

1. The children are told that the leader will alternate four movements: skipping, galloping, running, and walking. They are to follow every change of movement. The leader does not change direction unless he must.

2. The children follow the leader as closely as possible without bumping each other. The leader uses the movements enumerated in 1, but he also changes direction abruptly.

3. The children are divided into groups of three. Since fewer children can follow more closely, more intricate movements are used. For example, the leader might stop suddenly, crouch, hold his arms sideways, or walk on all fours. Whatever movement he uses, his followers must imitate. If the available area is small, no more than two groups should participate at a time, the others engaging in another activity.

4. Advanced children should coordinate their movements so that they form a close group moving in a smooth sequence and using a main theme, such as a forward movement low to the ground, forward and circular movements at the middle level, or running and leaping as high as possible.

Agility – 7

Forward Somersaults

The teacher must ensure that the children do this properly so as to avoid any possible injury to the neck muscles. An inexperienced or young child often attempts to straighten his neck just before rolling so that the body weight is borne on the neck instead of the shoulders. The teacher should at first assist the child by placing one hand on the child's buttocks and the other on the nape of the neck, lifting the child over and down while at the same time keeping the child's head tucked under.

1. The children lie facedown on the floor, heads resting on folded arms. They raise themselves on their toes and "walk" forward, keeping their arms in the same position and on the same spot. They tuck the head down to the chest while "walking" and finally roll over.

2. The children kneel. They place their hands on the floor, raise the buttocks, and roll over by pushing with toes and knees. The head is tucked under the chest.

3. The children squat, hands on the floor midway between front and sides. They push the body forward with the feet and roll over.

4. The children somersault and come to their feet in a single movement by rolling over rapidly and then thrusting the arms out to get the weight as far forward as possible.

5. The children practice backward and forward somersaults and sideway rolls.

6. Each child tries to develop a movement sequence using a backward or forward somersault or sideway roll, combined with walking, running, turning, or a combination of these movements.

Agility — 8

Tumbling

When the children have learned to perform simple somersaults, a variety of simple tumbling exercises may be introduced. They include somersaults from a running start, somersaults finishing in a standing position, and doing a handstand and then rolling over. In the last exercise, the teacher should support children as they roll over.

If the teacher wants to integrate tumbling into the program beyond the level of such simple movements, she needs training in teaching these skills, which may be enjoyed by some of the older and more advanced children.

Inexperienced teachers should not use this exercise or other tumbling exercises. Careful observation and skillful assistance are necessary.

Agility — 9

Kneeling to Standing

1. The children kneel on the floor, arms hanging at the sides. They rise to a standing position in any way they want but as quickly as possible. If necessary, they may support themselves with one hand on the floor.

2. As 1, but the children fold their arms in front of the chest and do not use their hands for assistance.

3. The children kneel with toes bent toward the body. They stand up in one quick movement by rolling the weight onto the balls of the feet and straightening the legs. They may not use the hands, and the feet remain anchored. If necessary, a partner may at first support the hands lightly.

Agility — 10

STRENGTH (Arm muscles)

Lying to Standing

The children lie facedown on the floor, hands beside the shoulders with palms on the floor and elbows bent. They stand up by pushing on the floor with their hands and jumping up. If they cannot jump up, they should scramble up quickly in any way they can.

Agility — 11 (Body awareness)

Sitting to Standing

1. The children sit on the floor, knees bent, feet flat. They wrap their arms around their knees, pull forward, get up to a standing position, and then stand still.

If necessary, they may assist themselves by momentarily placing a hand on the floor, but they should manage without this help as soon as possible.

2. As 1, but the children sit tailor-fashion. They get up with their legs crossed.

3. Two children sit in the same position as in 1 but facing each other and holding hands. They stand up and sit down together, giving each other support.

4. The children sit in pairs back to back, their arms linked, feet flat on the floor. At the teacher's signal, they rise to a standing position, assisting each other by pushing against the other's back. They return to the original position in the same way.

Agility — 12
STRENGTH (Leg muscles)
BALANCE (Static)

Launching the Rocket
From a crouch position, the children jump into the air, stretching their bodies and arms as far upward as possible. They land upright on their feet and stand still.

Agility — 13
STRENGTH (Leg muscles)
Duck Walk
The children waddle forward in crouch position. They hold their hands flat together behind their backs, fingers pointing away from the body to form a duck's tail.

This exercise should not be used for any extensive time, as it may overstrain the leg muscles. The teacher should have the children shake their legs after doing the exercise.

Agility — 14
STRENGTH (Abdominal muscles)
Threshing Machine
The teacher should explain and show illustrations of a threshing machine before the lesson.

1. The children lie on one side, arms and legs stretched forward at right angles to the trunk. They roll over to the other side, keeping their arms and legs in the same relationship to the trunk.

2. As 1, but the children bend arms and knees.

3. As 2, but the children try to gain momentum as they swing their bodies three times to the right and three times to the left. At the end of the third swing, they use the momentum to roll onto their bellies and rise quickly to a standing position.

Agility — 15

Log-Ball-Log

1. The children lie at full length on the floor, arms stretched above their heads, and roll over and over sideways in any direction (log rolling).

2. The children lie on their sides on the floor and then curl up with knees and elbows bent, head tucked down as close to the knees as possible. They roll in this position.

3. The children change back and forth from a "ball" to a "log" — that is, curl and uncurl the body quickly several times while rolling on the floor.

4. As 3, but the children change the direction and tempo of rolling.

Agility — 16

COORDINATION

Skipping

1. The children practice skipping without a partner. They may skip in any direction or pattern — forward, backward, diagonally, in a circle, in a square, and so on. They must take care not to collide with others.

2. The children skip in pairs, holding hands.

3. The children stand side by side in pairs, arms crossed and hands joined in front. They skip freely in pairs, changing direction frequently but avoiding collisions with other children.

4. The children change from skipping to galloping and back again at the teacher's signal. This can be done singly or in pairs.

5. Three children hold hands forming a circle; two children face in, the other out. The child facing out is the leader or "horse." The children run together trying to progress smoothly and staying at the same distance from each other. At a signal they begin to skip, keeping the same formation.

6. As 1, but either at a signal from the teacher or when they want, the children make a 180 degree turn by jumping and turning in the air, without pause, then skip in the opposite direction.

7. The children practice skipping backward and sideways (which is quite difficult) while facing ahead. Then they change the directions in which they skip.

8. The children practice mixing big steps with their skipping.

9. The children develop movement sequences involving skipping, walking, running, and turning. They demonstrate their sequences to each other and discuss them.

Agility — 17

Airplane

1. From a crouch position, the children jump into the air with arms outstretched and legs together, as an airplane taking off. They run, arms still outstretched, bending to make turns, avoiding imaginary thunderstorms and other airplanes. They can change "altitude" by bending and straightening the trunk or by bending the knees.

2. The teacher explains what formation flying is. The children are divided into groups of three. They take off as groups, fly high, then low, then in zigzag patterns, three children moving in unison. They change their movement at the teacher's signal.

3. Each child develops his own stunt flying sequence.

4. As 2, but one child is slightly ahead and acts as the leader. The others must follow his movements.

5. As 1 or 4, but the airplanes have to avoid crashing into "mountains," cards set up as obstacles by the teacher.

Agility — 18

STRENGTH (Leg muscles)

Kangaroo Hop

The children crouch, fingers touching the floor between their knees. They jump up and forward, bodies stretched, and land in a crouch position again.

At first the children should proceed in this way for short distances only, but the distances may be gradually increased as the movement becomes familiar.

Agility — 19 (Eye-foot coordination)

Swing and Jump

The children form a circle about 15 feet in diameter. One child stands in the middle and swings an 8- to 10-foot rope with a beanbag or a fluffy ball on the end of it in a circle a few inches from the ground. Each child jumps over the ball or beanbag as it reaches him.

The teacher should swing the rope if this is too difficult for any of the youngsters.

Strength

The exercises in this section were devised specifically for strengthening muscles. For example, exercises that involve lifting the weight of the body, such as jumping, chinning, and push-ups, enhance strength specifically. But since any movement provides exercise for some muscle or muscles, every activity in the movement education program contributes to the strengthening of muscle groups, whatever its prime purpose.

Many exercises on apparatus develop strength particularly. Arm strength, for example, is developed by climbing a jungle gym, a rope, a pole, or rungs without using the feet; by traversing parallel bars or horizontal ladders (on top of them, supported by arms, or hanging below them); by swinging from bars, rings, or a trapeze; and by a handstand on the bars. Leg strength can be developed by jumping from or vaulting over apparatus; by rope or pole climbing, using the legs; by hanging from bars by the legs; and so on.

Some of the following exercises require the greatest muscle strength during the execution of the movement; others require the greatest strength in achieving the final position. For example, when a child lies on his back and slowly raises his legs, the strongest pull on the muscles is exerted when the legs are a few inches from the floor; when he is asked to touch his toes, the strongest pull is when he is in the final position. In the first type, the exercises can often be made more difficult by requiring the children to perform them at a slower tempo; in the second type, by requiring them to hold the final position. In either case, care should be taken to avoid over-exertion. It is better to have the children repeat the exercises during a number of movement education periods at a reasonably comfortable level than it is to let them feel strain.

Strength – 1 (Leg muscles)
FLEXIBILITY (Ankles)
Feathering
1. The children stand about three feet from a wall, touching the wall with arms extended parallel to the floor. They bend their feet and toes toward the shins as far as possible; then on tiptoe. They should practice the movement. (They are told that this movement in the ankles propels the body upward in jumping. We call it "feathering" because it enables them to jump as lightly as feathers.)

2. The children make small jumps from a standing position, keeping their feet together and knees straight. Their toes are pointed toward the floor as they jump.

Strength — 2 (Thigh muscles)

Elevator

The children adopt an upright kneeling position, thighs vertical, backs straight. They slowly sit down on their calves, keeping their backs straight, and then rise to the upright position again. Repeat.

If a child has difficulty, he can perform the exercise with a partner. The children kneel opposite each other and do the exercise holding hands.

Strength — 3 (Thigh muscles)

Seesaw Knee Bends

Ordinary knee bends may overstrain the knees. Seesaw knee bends avoid this difficulty and at the same time strengthen the calf muscles.

Two children stand facing each other, holding hands. One does a knee bend. He comes up, slightly assisted by his partner, who is going down. They continue to sink and rise alternately. As they perform the movement, the children sing "See, saw, Margery Daw."

Strength — 4 (Abdominal muscles)
AGILITY

Shoulder Stand

The children lie on their backs on the floor. They raise the legs (with knees bent), pelvis, and lower trunk from the floor until the weight is resting on the shoulders, neck, head, and the backs of the upper arms. The hands should support the body at the waist.

Strength — 5 (Leg, abdominal muscles)

The Leg Piston

1. The children lie on their backs. They move their legs in a piston-like movement, bringing one knee back toward the chest as the other is held straight out and on the floor. The raised knee should be brought back as close to the chest as possible.

2. As 1, but the children return the piston leg and hold it off the floor up to the count of three and then rest it on the floor.

This child needs help in straightening his legs as he does the shoulder stand. The exercise helps strengthen the trunk muscles.

Strength — 6 (Thigh, trunk muscles)

Raising Leg Sideways

1. The children lie on their sides, the bottom arm stretched straight up, the head resting on it. The top arm is bent at the elbow in front of the body, the palm of the hand squarely on the floor to support the body in the following movements and to keep it in position. The top leg is raised and lowered slowly. The exercise is then repeated, lying on the other side and raising the other leg.

2. As 1, but the children move the raised leg in circles, first clockwise then counterclockwise.

3. As 1, but the children move the raised leg in as many ways as they can devise.

Strength — 7 (Back muscles)
FLEXIBILITY

Look at Me

The children lie facedown, hands clasped behind neck. They slowly raise head and chest as high as possible, keeping them in a straight line. Then they slowly lower them. If a child has difficulty in keeping his lower trunk and legs on the floor, another child can hold down his ankles.

After exercises in which the spine is bent backward, exercises with forward bending need to follow. See Chapter 4, Isometric Exercise 8.

Strength — 8 (Lower back muscles)
FLEXIBILITY (Abdominal muscles)

Legs Up
The children lie facedown, arms outstretched to the sides. They raise
the legs and lower trunk as high as possible, keeping them straight.
If a child has difficulty in keeping his chest on the floor, another
child can hold down his shoulders.

 After exercises in which the spine is bent backward, exercises
with forward bending need to follow. See Chapter 4, Isometric Exercise 8.

Strength — 9 (Back, neck, shoulder muscles)
FLEXIBILITY

Rocking Horse
The children lie facedown, arms outstretched to the sides or overhead.
They raise arms, neck, head, and legs as high as possible from the

Walking the middle rail of the parallel bars can be done by beginners.

floor. They then rock back and forth.

After exercises in which the spine is bent backward, exercises with forward bending need to follow. See Chapter 4, Isometric Exercise 8.

Strength – 10 (Abdominal muscles)
Making a Right Angle
The children lie faceup, raise their legs slowly until they are vertical, and then lower them slowly. The legs should be straight, and the head and shoulders flat on the floor. Some children may need to raise one leg at a time to get both off the floor and parallel.

Strength – 11 (Abdominal muscles)
FLEXIBILITY
Sit-Ups
The children lie faceup, arms at sides, knees bent. They sit up without using their hands and lean forward to touch their toes. Repeat three to five times. If the exercise is too difficult for a child, a partner can hold down his ankles.

Strength – 12 (Arm, shoulder muscles)
Bobbing for Apples (Half push-ups)
The children kneel, hands on the floor, arms straight, back parallel to the floor. They bend their arms until the chest is on the floor, allowing the feet to rise. They hold up to the count of three and then return to the original position.

Strength – 13 (Abdominal muscles)
FLEXIBILITY (Spine)
Sit-Ups with Bent Knees
The children lie faceup, arms at the sides, knees bent. They sit up without using their hands, put their arms around their knees, and curl up tight, head touching knees. Repeat five times. A partner can hold the feet down if necessary.

Strength – 14 (Leg muscles)
AGILITY
FLEXIBILITY (Spine backward)
BALANCE (Dynamic)
Russian Dance Jump
1. The children make small feathering jumps, keeping the knees straight.

2. As 1, but at every third jump the children bring the knees as near to the chest as possible.

3. As 1, but at every jump the children bend their knees and touch their heels during the jump. They should land lightly.

Strength — 15 (Shoulder girdle, arm, back muscles)
COORDINATION
BALANCE (Object)

Circus Seal Walk

1. The children lie facedown. They place their hands by their shoulders and straighten their arms to raise the upper part of the body. They move forward, walking on the hands only and dragging the legs, which should stay straight and together.

2. To include balancing in the exercise and to induce the children to hold their heads high, the children carry a beanbag on the head.

3. The teacher should show pictures of a circus act with seals and ask the children to devise their own tricks. For example, they might turn to a position lying on their sides, with the beanbag still balanced, or they might push the upper body in the air as a seal does when he is thrown a fish.

Strength — 16 (Arm, back, abdominal muscles)
FLEXIBILITY

Inchworm

The children lie facedown with hands near the shoulders and the balls of the feet on the floor. They straighten their arms, raising the trunk until it is approximately parallel to the floor, supported on hands and feet. Keeping the knees straight, they walk forward with small steps until the feet are as near to the hands as possible. Then they move the hands forward step by step until the trunk is again parallel to the floor. The movement pattern is repeated so that the children move slowly forward.

Strength — 17 (Leg, abdominal muscles)

Karate Kick

The children lie faceup and slowly raise their legs over the head until they are parallel with the floor. The hips are supported by the hands. The children return to a sitting position by swinging the legs down in a rapid motion, and at the same time raising the head and back. They should try not to help themselves with their hands.

Flexibility

Flexibility exercises emphasize the maximum extension of movement in the joints and stretching the muscles. Flexibility is the prime attribute required in acrobatics. The purpose in this program is not, however, to train acrobats but simply to maintain the flexibility that is characteristic of young children.

Poor flexibility and poor posture are frequently found together. These exercises help children to maintain range of movement and to achieve good posture.

Several approaches can readily be used for promoting flexibility — for example, weaving between the bars of a jungle gym, turning over while suspended from rings, and turning on the parallel bars. (Many exercises for agility also train flexibility. For example, Agility Exercise 7, Forward Somersaults, provides excellent training in flexibility.)

Flexibility Cues

The teacher should ensure that the children stretch their muscles smoothly and slowly to the point where they become aware of effortful extension. That point should be held for about five seconds. The children should not "bounce" in an attempt to extend the range; if they do, there is danger of muscle tear. For example, a child should not bounce up and down in an attempt to touch his toes.

Each flexibility exercise should be repeated for a minimum of three times.

Flexibility — 1 (Shoulder joints)
STRENGTH (Shoulder girdle muscles)
Arm Circles
1. The children sit with their arms stretched out to the sides. Keeping their backs straight, they make small backward circular movements with the arms, gradually increasing the size of the circles. They should feel the movement pulling the shoulder blades back.
2. As 1, but the children stand.
3. As 2, but the children circle their arms in varying tempos and hold them out at different angles from the body — in front, sideways, above the head, or reaching backward as far as possible. They may lean the trunk in the direction of the arms. The feeling should be one of reaching out and extending the personal space. The arms may be parallel or in different directions. Each child should develop the movements as freely as possible.

Flexibility — 2 (Spine; leg muscles)

The Bell

1. The children stand with feet apart, arms relaxed at the sides. They bend forward, keeping the knees stiff, and touch the floor. They grasp their ankles and pull steadily, trying to bend down as much as possible. They then return to the original position.

2. As 1, but when in the bent position the children pretend to be big bells and swing their arms and trunk forward and backward. The swing of the arms helps to raise and lower the upper part of the body.

3. As 2, but after swinging forward and backward a few times, the children use the upward swing as impetus for a jump (feet together) or leap (legs extended). They may progress across the room in this fashion.

Flexibility — 3 (Spine; leg muscles)

Head to Foot

The children sit on the floor, legs spread and flat. They lean forward, grasp one ankle with both hands, and pull the head down toward the leg, which is kept flat on the floor. Repeat, alternating sides.

Flexibility — 4 (Hips and legs)

Ankle Hold Walk

The children bend forward, keeping knees straight, grasp ankles, and walk forward. If this is too difficult, the children should first do the exercise holding their calves.

Flexibility — 5 (Spine; leg muscles)
COORDINATION (Crossing the midline)

The Train

1. The children sit on the floor, legs straight and as far apart as is comfortable. They slide a beanbag forward and back to the thigh of each leg alternately, bending forward as far as possible while keeping the knees straight.

2. As 1, but the children stretch both arms high above the head. They bend forward as far as possible toward the right and left foot alternately, keeping the arms in line with the trunk and the knees straight.

3. As 2, but without the beanbag.

4. As 2, but in standing position.

Flexibility – 6 (Spine)
COORDINATION (Arm, leg movements)
BALANCE (Dynamic)

Elephant Walk

The children link the fingers of both hands and bend forward at the waist, letting the arms swing loosely. They take a heavy step with the right foot, swinging the arms to the right; then a heavy step with the left foot, swinging the arms to the left. They continue walking in this way. The swinging motion should pull the body forward.

Flexibility – 7 (Spine; hips)
BALANCE (Static)

The Acrobat

1. The children sit on the floor. They make a sling for one knee with both hands and try to pull the knee to the forehead.

2. Children who can do 1 may attempt the same thing while standing on one foot.

Flexibility – 8 (Hips and legs)

Leg Stretch

1. The children lie faceup on the floor. They raise one leg as high as possible, keeping the knee straight and the other leg on the floor. They lower the raised leg and repeat with the other leg.

2. The children raise one leg as far up and back as possible and then move it forward and backward with small movements, each time trying to pull the leg a little closer to the head. These should be smooth movements with slightly stronger and weaker pulls alternating. The knees stay straight. Repeat with the other leg.

Flexibility – 9 (Hips and legs)
BALANCE (Static)

Leg Lift

1. The children stand with feet parallel and slightly apart. They slowly raise one leg forward as high as possible and then slowly lower it, keeping the legs and the back as straight as possible. Repeat with the other leg. If the children have difficulty in maintaining balance, they may use a chair or railing or the hand of another child for support.

2. As 1, but the children raise each leg sideways as far as possible.

3. As 1, but the children raise each leg backward. Since many children have a backward curvature of the spine, it is suggested that this be done cautiously.

Flexibility — 10 (Spine; hip joints)
BALANCE (Static)
Leg Swing
1. The children stand upright and swing one leg back and forth. Repeat with the other leg.
2. As 1, but the children swing each leg sideways.
3. As 1, but the children make circles with each leg.
4. As 1, but the children swing each leg far out in front so that it forces them to take a forward step. They continue with these "giant" steps across the room or in a circle.

Flexibility — 11 (Spine)
STRENGTH (Abdominal muscles)
The Drawbridge
The children lie on the floor faceup. They slowly raise their legs, keeping them straight, and lower them over the head until their toes touch the floor; then they slowly return to the starting position.

This exercise is easier when the children bend their elbows and push with their hands against the floor, keeping the hands close to the body.

Flexibility — 12 (Spine)
STRENGTH (Abdominal muscles)
Rocking Somersaults
1. The children sit on the floor, knees bent, arms around them. They rock backward until their shoulders touch the floor; they rock forward until their feet touch the floor.
2. As 1, but the children stretch out the legs and keep arms at the sides of the body. Stretching the arms forward as the children rock forward may help to bring the body up to sitting position.
3. As 2, but the children swing their legs all the way back and over the head, touching the floor with their toes.
4. As 3, but the children pull their knees toward the head and roll completely over, finishing in a kneeling position.

Flexibility — 13 (Hip joints)
STRENGTH (Trunk muscles)
BALANCE (Dynamic, static)
Ballet Dancer
1. The children crouch and sit back on their heels, back straight, fingers laced behind the neck. They bend the head and upper trunk

sideways to right and left alternately without leaning forward.

2. As 1, but the children are in an upright kneeling position.

3. As 2, but the children have one leg stretched out to the side.

4. The children perform the exercise in a standing position, with the weight almost entirely on one leg, the other stretched sideways with only the toes touching the floor.

5. The children try to walk, turn, twist, and bend while as high on their toes as possible. Each develops his own movement sequence.

Flexibility – 14 (Spine)

Hiding the Head

The children sit with knees bent and feet flat on the floor. They bend the trunk forward until the head touches the knees. They slide the feet farther apart, circle the knees with the arms, and lower the head between the knees as far as they can. They then sit up straight again. Repeat two to four times.

Flexibility – 15 (Spine)

BALANCE (Static)

Windshield Wipers

1. The children sit on the floor with their legs straight in front. They place their hands on their hips and turn as far as possible to the right without turning the knees inward or bending forward. The children should turn as far as possible without falling. Repeat to the left and then alternate in a smooth, continuous motion.

2. As 1, but the children's arms are stretched parallel above the head.

3. As 1, but the children are standing.

Flexibility – 16 (Spine; leg muscles)

Writing Behind

The children stand bent forward with feet wide apart. They reach back through their legs as far as possible and make a mark on the floor with a piece of chalk. At each attempt they try to make a more distant mark.

Flexibility – 17 (Spine)

RELAXATION

Head Circles

1. The children sit cross-legged and rotate their heads in as large

circles as possible, first clockwise and then counterclockwise. The movements should be very slow for maximum stretch. The trunk and shoulders remain still.

2. As 1, but the children rotate the upper body and shoulders as well as the head.

Flexibility — 18 (Spine)
COORDINATION
AGILITY
BALANCE (Static)

Through the Tunnel and Over the Bridge
In each of the three variations, the speed with which the ball is passed should gradually be increased so that agility and balance are also involved.

1. The children stand in single file, legs apart, to form a tunnel. The front child passes a large ball between his legs to the child behind, who passes it to the child behind him, and so on to the end of the line.

2. The children pass the ball backward over their heads. They should stand fairly far apart so that backward extension is required.

3. The children pass the ball through the tunnel and overhead, alternately.

Flexibility — 19 (Trunk)
AGILITY
BALANCE (Static)

Over the Stile
1. Each child grasps a 30-inch rod by both ends and holds it in front of him at about hip level, parallel to the ground. He steps over it, first with one foot and then with the other. Repeat a few times.

2. The children are asked to find another way of getting the rod behind them without releasing one end. (The solution is to move it over the head. See Flexibility Exercise 20.)

Flexibility — 20 (Shoulder girdle)

Train Gate
1. The children stand with legs apart. Each grasps a 30-inch rod at both ends and raises it slowly over the head and as far back as possible, keeping the arms straight and trunk upright. Then they bring the rods slowly back to the front. The rods should always be horizontal.

2. As 1, but the children sit with legs straight.

Flexibility – 21 (Spine)

The Rocking Chair

1. The children sit on the floor, knees close to the chest, arms around knees, head bent forward, feet off the floor. They roll forward and backward.

2. From rolling forward as in 1, some children may be able to gain enough momentum to swing up to a standing position by thrusting their arms forward.

Flexibility – 22 (Spine)
AGILITY

Back Roll

1. The children lie on the floor faceup. They raise their legs overhead with knees bent and bring their knees down on either side of the head as close to the floor as possible. They roll backward to a sitting position. The children have their arms at their sides and may push on the floor with their hands.

2. As 1, but the children try to do the exercise without pushing on the floor.

Flexibility – 23 (Hip joints)
BALANCE (Static)

Step Through the Ring

1. The children stand straight and lace their fingers together and make a ring with their arms. They pull one knee up to the chest, keeping the other leg and the back as straight as possible, although the head and neck may be bent forward. They maintain the position up to the count of three.

2. As 1, but the children step through the ring, first with one leg and then with the other. (This is an advanced variation.)

Flexibility – 24 (Spine)

The Cat

The children assume a crawling position, hands and knees on the floor and back horizontal. They round the back like an angry cat, pulling the head toward the trunk. They straighten the neck and let the spine slowly sink to resting position.

Flexibility – 25 (Spine; hip joints)
STRENGTH (Trunk muscles)

The Mermaid

1. The children lie on their sides. They place the hand of the top

arm on the floor in front of the chest for support. They raise both legs sideways as high as possible, keeping the legs together.

2. The children lie on their sides, arms stretched above the head. They raise their legs and the upper part of the body as high as possible and rock up and down on the pivot of the hip, rocking on the waves.

Balance

Fine adjustment of weight, and therefore of muscle groups, is necessary in each of the three forms of balance. Balance exercises also contribute to body awareness, and they are therefore particularly useful.

If a child has difficulty in maintaining static balance, he should at first be allowed to help himself by holding onto an object, such as a chair, or by holding another child's hand. When he can do the exercise in this way, he should release the support and try to maintain balance without it. Then he can attempt an exercise without support from the beginning.

Balance — 1 (Static)

Standing on Tiptoe
For all tiptoe positions, the heels should be raised from the floor as far as possible.

1. The children stand, raise themselves to tiptoe position, hold for three to five seconds, and then return to standing position.

2. As 1, but as the children rise on the toes they slowly raise a ball high overhead, using both hands.

Balance — 2 (Static)
COORDINATION

The Scale (Sideways balance)
The teacher explains to the children what a scale is and demonstrates how it is used to weigh things. She should proceed slowly with the following exercise, going step by step and demonstrating each new movement and position.

1. The children sit on the floor with legs straight and slightly apart, arms stretched sideways at right angles to the body, a position that resembles a scale. The children bend slowly and rhythmically right and left, keeping the arms at the same angle to the trunk and the back straight.

2. As 1, but the children bend right and left as far as possible.

3. The children stand with feet slightly apart, arms at right angles to the body. Keeping the hips as motionless as possible, they bend sideways as far as possible, first to one side and then to the other.

4. As 3, but at the same time the children raise sideways the leg on the side opposite to the direction of tilt. As the left arm goes up, the left leg goes up also and vice-versa.

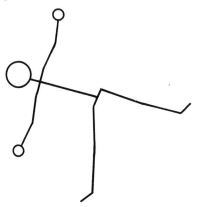

The teacher might say to the children:

(1)   "Today you are each going to be a scale, or balance. First, sit on the floor with your legs straight and a little bit apart like this (demonstrate). Good. Now put your arms out to the sides to make the scale. Fine.

"Now we are going to weigh some apples. We put some apples on the right side, and the right arm goes slowly down like this (demonstrate). Then we put weights on the left side of the scale, and the left arm goes down like this (demonstrate). Now you do that. Don't move your shoulders at all. Keep your arms straight out to the sides and bend your back so that your arms go up and down. Fine. Now we will put more apples and more weights on the scale so that you keep tilting from side to side like this (demonstrate). Keep going smoothly. Very good!

(2)   "Now a whole lot of apples are put on the scale, and they pull you way over to one side. See how low you can bend. Keep your arms straight and your hips still. Fine. Now the other way. Keep going from side to side, bending as low as you can. Good!

(3)   "Now can you be tall scales? Stand with your feet a bit apart. Put your arms out to the sides again. Now bend from side to side again. Good. Keep your arms in the same position and let them follow your body. Don't lean forward. Lean only to one side. See how far you can go.

(4)   "This time you are going to do a trick. When you lean over

to the left side like this (demonstrate), see if you can raise your right leg sideways like this (demonstrate). Then you'll do the same thing on the other side. Try it. Good!"

Balance — 3 (Static)
FLEXIBILITY

Forward Balance

1. The children stand on one foot and bend forward, raising the free leg backward until the trunk and free leg are parallel to the floor. They hold the arms at right angles to the body. The position is held to the count of three. Then they return to the standing position. Repeat, raising the other leg.

2. As 1, but the children raise the arms in front.

3. The children try to balance on one leg with the trunk and arms in any position they devise. They may be bent backward, sideways, or forward, and the arms may be in any symmetrical or asymmetrical position.

4. The children create movement sequences by adopting the original balance position, taking a few steps, adopting another position, and so on, finishing with the original position. Repeat the sequence.

Balance — 4 (Static)

One-Leg Swing

1. The children balance on one foot and swing the free leg forward and backward twice. They balance on each foot alternately.

2. As 1, but the children swing the free leg to the side and back again.

3. The children swing the free leg forward, then out to the side, and then in and forward again in a rhythmic motion. Repeat up to five times.

4. As 3, but the children swing the free leg to the side and then in and slightly backward. (To avoid swayback, the backward swing should not be emphasized.)

Balance — 5 (Static)
STRENGTH (Abdominal, leg muscles)

Making a V

The children sit on the floor, legs together and straight, arms outstretched parallel to the floor. They raise their legs as high as possible, keeping them straight, maintaining balance on the buttocks without using hand support.

Balance — 6 (Static)

STRENGTH (Abdominal, thigh muscles)

The Bicycle

1. The children lie faceup. They raise their legs and lower trunk as nearly vertical as possible, the weight on the back of the shoulders and the hands supporting the upper body. They make bicycling movements with their legs.

2. As 1, but the children move their legs back and forth like scissors, keeping the legs straight.

3. From the faceup position, the children slowly raise their legs up and overhead, keeping them straight and close together, until their feet touch the floor behind the head. They reach a sitting position by swinging the legs quickly back to the floor, at the same time raising the head and back.

Balance — 7 (Object)

Water Carriers

The teacher should explain that in some dry countries, the women fetch water from the wells, carrying the jars on their heads. She should also show pictures.

In the first four variations, each child carries a beanbag representing a water jar on his head. In Variations 5 and 6, he carries the beanbag elsewhere. He tries not to spill the water.

1. The children walk along various paths: forward, backward, sideways, or in various directions, twisting and turning.

2. The children change speed while walking, becoming slower and faster.

3. The children are told to find different ways of moving about, such as skipping, running, or walking on tiptoe.

4. The children make up different combinations of movements and turns.

5. As 1-3, but the children find other parts of the body on which to carry the beanbag. For example, one child may choose the back of the neck, another the crook of the arm, and still another the top of his folded arms.

6. As 5, but the children are in different body positions. For example, one child crouches low, another moves on his knees, another on all fours, and another on tiptoe.

Balance — 8 (Object)

Carry the Marble

1. The children walk to a goal, carrying a marble or small ball on a spoon.

2. As 1, but the children run.

3. The children may race after they practice 1 and 2.

4. As 1, but the children walk blindfolded.

5. The children interlace the fingers of their hands and hold them palms down in front of and away from the chest or abdomen. The marble is balanced on top of the hands. The children try to walk, change direction, turn, jump, skip without letting the marble fall.

6. Two children face each other. They form a tray by putting their four hands together, backs upward. They try to carry a marble on the tray, one child walking backward, the other forward.

Balance – 9 (Dynamic)
STRENGTH (Calf muscles)

Giraffe Walk

The children stretch their arms overhead and clasp their hands together, forming a giraffe's head and neck. They imitate the giraffe's movement by walking on tiptoe with legs stretched and knees stiff. The arms and trunk may sway slightly, but they must always point upward.

Balance – 10 (Dynamic)

Balance Beam

There are many patterns and movements that children may use to traverse a balance beam. Patterns may be combined with different arm positions, such as stretched sideways, folded across the chest, or straight in front. After the children have mastered the basic movements, they should be encouraged to devise new patterns.

1. The children walk forward and backward on the beam.

2. They walk sideways; then they walk sideways in both directions, first crossing one leg behind the other, then crossing one leg in front of the other.

3. They practice turning.

4. They skip, hop, or jump along.

Most of the following stunts may be done while going backward, forward, or even sideways on the beam.

5. The children walk two steps forward, make a half-turn, walk two steps sideways, make a half-turn, and walk two steps forward. Repeat, turning in the opposite direction.

6. They walk two steps backward, make a quarter-turn, slide two steps sideways, make a quarter-turn, and take two steps backward. Repeat, turning in the opposite direction.

7. They walk with bent knees.

8. They walk, swinging the free leg far forward before taking a step.

9. They walk four steps forward and drop to knee-bend position.

10. They walk forward, raising the knees as high as possible.

11. They alternate small and big steps.

12. They stand, squat, sit down. Repeat.

13. They walk on tiptoe; walk on heels.

14. They slide along the beam, one foot behind the other.

15. They skip across the beam.

16. They cross the beam on hands and feet; use both hands and one foot.

17. They crawl forward, backward, and sideways.

18. They throw and catch a beanbag or ball while crossing.

19. One child walks backward, the other forward; they hold hands.

20. They slide hands forward along the beam and jump over it from side to side.

21. They hop, cupping the free foot in the hands.

22. They cross using Tightrope Walk (Coordination Exercise 5).

23. They do stunts on a beam set at an angle.

These youngsters practice dynamic balance as they walk this course with arms outstretched.

Balance — 11 (Dynamic)

Balance Board

1. The children stand on balance boards, keeping them from tilting.

2. The children try to tilt the boards without falling, tilting the boards right and left, backward and forward, and with rolling motions.

Balance — 12 (Static, dynamic)
COORDINATION
AGILITY

Statues

1. The children stand on the floor and adopt a succession of positions, holding each for a few seconds. For example, they may stand on one foot or on tiptoe and move arms, legs, head, and trunk into various positions and into various relationships with each other. They then return to an upright position.

2. As 1, but the children stand on stools, beams, blocks, or low benches.

3. The teacher shows pictures of various positions and the children imitate them.

4. The children are paired, and one child adopts positions that the other imitates. The roles are reversed.

5. The children run in a circle while the teacher beats a percussion instrument. When the teacher stops, they adopt any position they can think of, but only one foot may touch the floor and the trunk may not be erect. After a count of five, the teacher again beats the instrument, and the children continue running.

6. The children jump, skip, or gallop in a circle according to the teacher's rhythmic signals; they drop into a crouch position when the rhythm ceases. They move forward again when the rhythm resumes.

7. As 6, but the children freeze in the crouch position for only an instant before resuming the flow of movement. They make the movement as smooth as possible.

Balance — 13 (Dynamic)
AGILITY
STRENGTH (Leg muscles)

Stepping Stones

The teacher places large blocks or discs close together on the floor.

1. The children step from one block or disc, or "stepping stone," to another. The distance between them is gradually increased.

2. The children step to the floor between their steps on the blocks and increase speed. They hold the position on each block briefly.

Discs can be used for many kinds of exercises. Here the children learn to balance on one foot.

If discs are used, the following exercises may be added:

3. The children jump from disc to disc, both feet together.

4. The children jump with one foot only, alternating, in as smooth a rhythm as possible.

5. The teacher arranges the stepping stones in an irregular pattern. The children cross a "river" on all fours without putting a hand or a foot in the "water."

6. The children cross the river in any manner they can devise. They may jump from stone to stone, turning in the air as they jump, for example. Or they may cross the river in pairs or in groups, holding hands and skipping, leaping, or running. Other children may help each other carefully across wide spaces between stones; or they may proceed wheelbarrow fashion. Each suggestion may elicit a variety of movement sequences.

7. Other objects may be introduced. For example, the children may cross the river while bouncing a ball on the stones; or they may throw a beanbag on top of the first stone, jump up on the stone, pick up the beanbag, throw it on top of the next stone, and so on.

Balance — 14 (Dynamic, static)

Whirl and Freeze (Turning with controlled motion)

1. The children rotate with a whirling motion sufficiently controlled to enable them to achieve a static position at a signal. When

the signal is given, they jump in the air, land in any position they choose, and remain still.

2. The teacher asks some of the children to repeat the movement patterns they have developed. The other children look on and try to copy each in turn.

3. Groups of two or three children join hands and form circles and then run or skip around. At a signal, the children jump in unison and then try to remain motionless in whatever position they land.

Speed

Speed of movement refers to the ability to sustain a continuous movement at a fast tempo. All running games, relay races, and, later on, timed runs may be used to provide training in speed. No exercises for speed as such are given in this program, although the attribute should be trained. Most exercises for coordination and agility may be used for training of speed, the teacher adapting the directions so that the children are required to use speed.

Relaxation

1. Head roll (Variation 1, Flexibility Exercise 17).

2. Shoulder roll (Variation 2, Flexibility Exercise 17).

3. The children sit with legs crossed and let the body droop forward in a relaxed position. They slowly rotate head, shoulders, and trunk, but they try not to shift the weight so much that they lose their balance.

4. The children lie on their backs, relaxed. They slowly raise their knees, letting the feet slide along the floor toward the trunk. They then relax the tension in the leg muscles and let the feet slide back to the original position.

5. As 4, but when the feet are near the trunk, the children let the knees and lower legs fall to the right so that they touch the floor. Then they swing them with as little effort as possible to the left, and so on from side to side in an easy motion, keeping the trunk relaxed on the floor.

6. The children lie on their backs, relaxed. They slowly raise their arms to a vertical position; then they relax the muscles and let the arms drop to the floor.

7. The children hold on to a rail, chair, or other fixed object and let one leg swing easily and freely.

8. The children relax the arm and leg muscles by shaking them. They may stand with the weight on one foot and shake the arms

and the free leg, or they may sit or lie down and shake their arms and legs.

9. The children lie on their backs, relaxed. They roll over lazily until they lie relaxed on the stomach; then they roll lazily back. They continue rolling back and forth in a relaxed manner.

10. The children lie on their backs, relaxed and with eyes closed. When the teacher names a body part, the children move it gently. She may say, for example, "Right little finger;" "Toes;" "Head;" "Left leg;" "Chin."

Breathing

1. The children stand upright with heads drooping and raise the arms horizontally, breathing in steadily while doing so and slowly lifting their heads. Then they lower the arms, letting the head droop again, and breathe out. Each child follows his own rhythm.

2. As 1, but the children sit cross-legged.

3. The children kneel, sitting on the heels, and bend forward in a relaxed position, head hanging near the floor. They breathe in steadily and at the same time straighten the back, raise the head, and rise to an upright kneeling position. The body is in a straight line from the knees to the top of the head. They then relax to the first position and at the same time breathe out. Each child follows his own rhythm..

4. The children lie on the floor faceup, hands on the abdomen. They breathe in and out steadily in their own rhythm. When breathing in they should feel the abdomen rise; when breathing out they should feel it sink.

5. The children lie on their backs on the floor and slide the arms sideways and up in a symmetrical movement until the heels of the hands meet overhead. As the children slide their arms up they breathe in; as they slide their arms back they breathe out.

Creative Movement

In helping children acquire a creative movement repertoire, only suggestions can be given to the children by the teacher. The suggestions may be used to start sessions, to introduce dimensions of movement to the children, and to combine various ideas in creating new movement sequences. The suggestions are in no way exhaustive, as the possible combination of movements is infinite, created by each child in his own way. A few examples of how such suggestions should be given by the teacher are included here.

Creative Movement – 1

Personal Space

The teacher tells the children to stand as far away from each other as possible so that they will not hinder each other in moving. They try to find out how far they can extend their arms and legs in all directions. The teacher describes the space around each child as his personal space – as a bubble surrounding him.

Children should be asked frequently to perform movements in their personal space.

Creative Movement – 2

Common Space

The children are told to run around the room, trying to realize how far it reaches in all directions. They must try to avoid bumping into each other while they are running. The teacher explains that the room has to be shared by everyone; it is called the common space.

Creative Movement – 3

Floor Patterns in the Common Space

The teacher tells the children to make various floor patterns without changing body direction. (Body direction changes each time the children face a different wall.) To illustrate, she uses a rope stretched in a wavy line on the floor. First the children run along beside the rope. After they understand what is meant by a floor pattern, they may move in straight lines, curves, and various combinations of these patterns, but always facing forward. Later they can explore how to move sideways, backward, in zigzags, and in circles, all without changing body direction.

Creative Movement – 4

Floor Patterns While Changing Body Direction

Each child stands by himself. The children are then told to walk floor patterns and to change body direction while doing so, going backward, forward, and sideways.

Creative Movement – 5

Shape

The children explore various shapes they can make with their bodies. They find out how their bodies can be narrow (like an arrow), wide and flat (like a wall), round (like a ball), or twisted (like a corkscrew).

They may change the shape of their bodies from one form to another. They combine various body positions into movement sequences.

Creative Movement — 6

Air Patterns

1. The teacher reminds the children of the floor patterns they can make and tells them that they can also make patterns in the air. They move heads, arms, and legs in different directions; they bend their trunks and move their bodies (without locomotion) in their personal space in as many different ways as they can devise.

2. The children are each given a ball large enough to clutch with both hands; they move the ball in the air so that it makes different patterns.

3. The children combine making air patterns with floor patterns.

Creative Movement — 7

Changes in Tempo

Each child moves in a circle, changing from walking very slowly to walking very quickly. Then each child makes different floor patterns, alternating quick and slow movements.

Creative Movement — 8

Changes in Weight

The children practice walking with heavy steps, then with light steps. They are told to make a big jump. The teacher points out how much force is needed to make a big jump and how little is needed to make a light jump. Using the Troll's Walk (Coordination Exercise 2), the children learn to make changes in the weight they use. If they vary the weight of movements, for example, by alternating one heavy step with three light ones, they can become aware that a movement sequence may have different accents.

Creative Movement — 9

Changes in Body Support

1. The children are helped to discover that their bodies can be supported on one, two, or more points. They explore how they can walk on four or three points, roll on the ground, hop on one foot, and so on.

2. Children practice transferring their weight from one body part to another, as, for instance, changing from standing to kneeling or going from a standing position to one on all fours.

Movements with various forms of body support should be practiced frequently.

Creative Movement — 10

Level

The children are told to make their movements in a high position (to walk on tiptoe). Later they walk in the medium position (normal standing position) and then choose a movement in the low position (close to the ground). They change from one position to another while moving around.

Creative Movement — 11

Flow

The concept of flow is difficult for young children, but as they progress in the program, they learn the difference between free, uncontrolled, swinging movements and well-controlled ones, such as those required in playing This Is It (Chapter 4). The concept of flow is most easily acquired in free dancing, swinging, and moving freely in every way until the children want to rest.

This type of movement should be alternated with controlled movements that require the children to stop immediately on a signal.

Creative Movement — 12

Changing Body Shape

In this exercise the shape of the body changes while the body is in motion; its level stays low.

1. The teacher may say, "Children, please lie on your backs. I challenge you* when I make a noise on the tambourine to roll up into a ball and then roll over so that you stay a ball. Stay very round and land on your knees. Fine! You are all doing very well. But let's watch John because he is so very, very round.

"Now let's all do it again. Lie straight on your back, make yourself into a ball, draw your knees up until they touch your chest, and then roll over. Okay, that was good. Now let's try it again."

2. This exercise can be reversed by having the children begin in a round position (head, knees, and arms touching the floor) and then having them turn around and land in the same round position but

---

*The word *challenge* is frequently used in creative movement. The teacher can give the children a challenge — a problem to solve. The word *challenge* is a suitable one when asking the children to do their best to solve a problem, but overuse — use with each exercise — may become trite and boring.

Above: In creative movement, children learn to make their bodies into many shapes — here a ball. Below: This little girl uses space differently — as a ballet dancer.

on the back. They stretch out and lie supine (on their backs) on the floor and then repeat the exercise.

3. The exercise may be combined with getting up as fast as possible after the children have reached the supine position; they should lie flat for an instant with head and whole body on the floor.

Creative Movement — 13

Using Space

1. "Please find the place where you usually stand during movement education. That's fine. You are all standing, and each has enough room for his personal space. First I would like you to make yourself as small as you can — take up as little space as you can. Try that. Fine. Most of you have chosen the shape of a ball, which is the smallest space your body can fill. Let's all do it again. Change the shape of your body into the shape of a ball."

2. "Now would you try to choose the position in which your body takes up as much space as possible? Fine. Most of you stretched your arms and legs out wide. But what did Philip do? Yes, you are right. He stood on one foot and stretched out one leg and both arms as far as he could. He certainly used a lot of space.

"When you were like balls you could have been very close to each other without disturbing your neighbors, but you can see that you need a lot of space when you are in a wide position."

3. "Now I suggest that you try to find out if you can change in a very slow way from the ball shape to one in which you need a lot of space. Try to show that you can expand slowly as a balloon, which at first is very small but then gets bigger and bigger as it is blown up. Okay? First the ball — very, very small. Now grow bigger and bigger. Fine. Stop. I think that Ellen and Jack can show us how they did it. They grew very slowly." A discussion of what the children saw should follow.

4. As 3, but three or four children stand close together in the middle of the room. As these children "expand," they do it in such a way that they reach out toward each other. The teacher may say, "When you were balls you were each by yourself. Now as you become bigger — as you expand your movement in space — you need more room. There are other children near you, and you have to be careful not to get in the way of the movements of the other children. As you expand as widely as possible, you may touch each other but not bump or push into each other. That's fine." Another group of children repeat the variation.

After all the children have done the variation, the teacher may suggest that the children discuss how close they can be to each other while taking the shape of a ball and still be far enough apart so that they can make the movements together. They should, in their final position, show that they are aware of the other children but are not restricting each other's movements.

Creative Movement – 14

Locomotion: One Direction, One Level
The low position is given as an example.

1. "Children, I challenge you to move forward in a very slow and round position close to the floor. Fine. Allan solved that problem by going forward in a kneeling position, John walked crouching, and Steven scooted on the floor in a sitting position. And Max! How did Max move? Would you show the other children? Fine. Yes, Max walked as a seal, pushing himself forward on his elbows.

"Now I challenge you to try some other ways. Try to imitate the way some of the other children have done it."

2. As 1, but the children move sideways in a low position, as, for instance, walking sideways in a crouch position or in a crawling position. Then they should change to different low positions and walk backward. At times they should try to have their faces up (crab walk position); at times they should turn their bodies sideways, one hand and both feet touching the floor during locomotion.

Other versions are (a) combine several movements into a sequence; (b) use locomotion on medium and high levels for the same exercises; and (c) do the exercises in pairs holding on to each other (especially important on an advanced level). For instance, one child in a bent position moves forward and the other in the pair, also in a bent position, moves backward, or both move sideways holding hands.

Creative Movement – 15

Changing Direction During Locomotion

1. Each child walks a floor pattern in any way he wants but in a high position, changing the direction of his body from time to time. The teacher says, "Fine, children. Remember, you went forward in space very high. Now try to change the direction in which you move when I make a sound on the tambourine, but stay very high. Okay?" The children continue, walking alternately in both high and low positions. They should discuss the floor patterns they made.

2. "I would now like you to change direction on a tambourine signal while walking a floor pattern in which you get as high as you can. Continue to move without stopping. Fine. What was Susie doing?

Yes, she leaped forward, and when I gave the signal for a change of direction she turned while leaping. Then she continued to leap without stopping. And what was Steven doing? Steven walked very high on his toes like a tightrope artist in a circus. When I touched the tambourine, he turned around and walked in another direction without wobbling. That was very good, Steven."

3. "This time I would like you to do the same as you did before, but I want you to do it in pairs so that when one child changes direction, the other child has to change with him. I suggest that at first you do not choose as difficult ways as some of you did before, but rather that you change direction in pairs while looking at each other. Walk first, perhaps, and then choose a different way of moving that is a little bit harder. Fine. Begin."

4. The teacher may have advanced children do the same in groups of three or four, and perhaps later in even larger groups.

Creative Movement – 16

Changing Direction of Movement Without
Changing the Direction in Which the Body Faces
After the children have learned to change the direction of movement during locomotion and have learned to walk floor patterns in high, low, and intermediate positions, they may do the following:

1. The teacher may say, "Let's stand in a big circle with one of you in the middle. Which one of you would like to be in the middle of the circle? All right, Mary. All face Mary while you first move in a high position as we did before. But sometimes move toward Mary and sometimes away from her to the outside of the circle. Try to move in a variety of ways. Some of you may be high, some may be low, some may be medium. Some of you go forward and some backward, but all of you should face Mary. That was good. Now, Janie, can you say what you did?" The children should discuss their different movements.

2. "Children, I challenge you to move in a high position but to change the direction in which you move without changing the direction in which your body faces when I make a sound on the tambourine. Don't forget, stay very high and always face in the same direction. Always look toward the windows. Okay? You may move sideways, but then you have to turn your head, don't you, to face the windows. You can walk forward and you can be high or you can be low or you can walk different floor patterns.

"What do you think you want to do, George? Yes, you can walk in a snake pattern – an *S* line. You can walk forward, then sideways, then forward again.

"Yes, you are right, Max, it would be like a stair drawn on the floor. (The teacher draws the pattern on the board.) All try to walk different floor patterns."

3. After the children have practiced this exercise, three to four children can walk in a group closely following a leader. The teacher may say, "Janie is the leader. You should all walk Janie's pattern. For instance, when Janie walks sideways to the right, you walk to the right; when she walks to the left, you walk to the left. Otherwise do it just as you did it before. That's a real challenge because you must change direction as fast as you can but walk slowly and with great caution because you are to be close. But don't bump each other."

Creative Movement — 17

Varying the Speed of Movement

1. "Lets's all go to our usual places and sit down and think a bit about a challenge. I challenge you to change your tempo while walking. Do you know what that means? Yes, you are right. It means to change the speed at which you walk. You can walk fast and then slow in any pattern you want. Each of you should do it in his own way, but don't bump into each other. Be careful in sharing the common space. Fine. That was very good."

2. "This time try to change the speed at which you walk and to change the level of the body at the same time. Will you try that? You can walk forward fast and at the same time become very tall, or you can walk forward fast and at the same time become very low — close to the floor. Remember, you have done this before. Try it again — first tall and fast, then tall and slow, then low and as fast as you can walk. Fine! Now you can move around any way you want — according to your own plan. Change the speed and the height of your body. Take up all the space in the gym, but no one should bump into anyone else.

"That was a real challenge, wasn't it? You did a fine job. Thank you."

Creative Movement — 18

Changing Body Position in Relation to an Object

An exercise such as the following can be done in relation to a geometric figure laid out with dowels or drawn on the floor, with a hoop, a rope, a beanbag, the leg of a chair, or with any other object the teacher chooses. The challenge is to relate either the whole body or part of the body to the object in a planned way.

1. "Each of you has a hoop. Can you put your head into the hoop — only your head? Fine. Now take your head out of the hoop and put an arm into it; now a foot; now an elbow. That was good. But now try to put your whole body in the hoop."

2. "This time I would like you to try to stay low to the floor and put your whole body in the hoop so that the top of your head and the bottom of your feet touch the hoop. You have to make yourselves quite small. Very good.

"Now let's look at how some of you did it. Jim laid on the floor and held the hoop with his feet and head. He was on his stomach, and he had to bend backward to do that well. Do you see how he did it? And Marge did it similarly, but she held the hoop with her feet and her head and put her arms into the hoop. That was a fine solution."

These children get ready to work together with the hoop on the floor.

First, each child puts a foot in the hoop while holding hands. Then each learns to put one foot and one hand in the hoop.

Last, they learn to solve the problem of how each can put his head in the hoop.

Creative Movement — 19

Changing Body Position in Relation to an Object (2)
This exercise may be done in the classroom.

1. "Look at this chair. I wonder if you can lie under the chair with your head sticking out on one side and your legs on the other side? Try it.

"Now I have three chairs so that three children should try to do it. Fine. That was easy. How did Jack and Bert do it? Jack lay on his stomach, and Bert lay on his back.

2. "Now I will give you a challenge. Without moving the chairs, each try to crawl in and out between the legs of his chair. Fine. That was very good. Some of the chairs did not wriggle at all. Try once more."

An exercise such as this should not be done by all the children at the same time, as that may cause too much moving of furniture or equipment, but it can be done with children who have learned to work in a circuit — several groups of children working at the same time but in different places in the gym or classroom. For instance, if the exercises are done in the classroom, one group of children may stay in their seats and practice moving their legs to a horizontal position and back to the floor again, strengthening their abdominal muscles. Another group may sit in a circle on their chairs, each child with a beanbag on his head. The children try not to let their beanbags fall while making various motions. A third group may weave in and out of the legs of a chair.

Creative Movement — 20

Chinese Rope Jumping — Relating the Body to Objects

Three children hold a long rope — one child holds the rope in the middle and the other two children hold the rope at each end. They hold it so that the two halves of the rope are parallel and horizontal and above the floor at the right height for children to jump over.

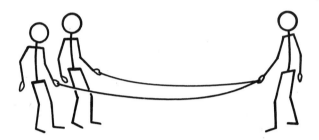

The teacher may give the following directions: "Today we are going to try to jump over a double rope, which is called Chinese rope jumping. Each of you should jump from one side of the rope into the middle — between the two strands — and then over to the other side. See how many ways you can do it."

The children find that they can jump on one or both feet, that they can turn around in the air while jumping, and so on. Each child should then try to create his own movement pattern.

Later the teacher should point out to the children that they can jump in such a way that both legs are outside both strands of rope so that they straddle it. They may jump between the two strands and out again in a variety of ways.

With advanced children, sensitivity to movement of one child to another is enhanced by having two children do an exercise together, trying variations.

Creative Movement — 21

Contact Between Pairs of Children

Creative movement enhances body awareness, one of its main goals. The following exercise and its variations give children a strong awareness of their bodies by having them create movements in pairs.

1. The children face each other in pairs holding hands and make side steps together across the room. The teacher may say, "Right, left; right, left; touch your left foot with the right foot," and correct whatever mistakes she observes.

2. The children sidestep in pairs as before, but they are told that each pair should proceed at its own pace and change directions while moving. The teacher may say, for instance, "That was very good. You all do the side step well. Now can you make different floor patterns, doing the same step all the time? Fine. You did a good job, but some of you moved only in straight lines. How would it be if you tried to alternate between curves and straight lines?"

After the children have tried modifications, the teacher may ask some children to show the others what they have done and have the children discuss the floor patterns. The teacher may point out how some children changed directions.

3. If the teacher feels the children are able to do it, she may add another variation, asking them to turn in a variety of ways while they change directions. They may, for instance, try to turn sharply, try to make a curve.

Creative Movement — 22

Changing Body Position While in Pairs

1. The children are told that the challenge is to go from a sitting position to a standing position while in pairs. Each pair should have contact with either one or both hands, and each pair should try various starting positions and various ways of holding on to each other. The teacher may say, "Be sure that you don't let loose while you are getting up. Try it."

After the children have practiced the exercise, they should show each other how they met the challenge. For instance, Jim and Jack sat side by side, legs bent at the knees, Jim to the right of Jack. They held hands and got up slowly, kneeling first and then standing up. They found that they had to be very near each other to be able to go from the sitting position to the kneeling position.

Chuck and Bob sat facing each other with legs crossed and holding each other's hands as they got up. Terence and Sue sat back to back with elbows hooked. They got up and sat down again, pressing their backs together and giving each other support. The children then tried each other's solutions.

2. As 1, but three or more children sit down, hold hands in a circle, and stand up and sit down together.

Creative Movement — 23

Moving with Eyes Closed and Led by Another Child

Body awareness and creativity may be greatly enhanced if one child with eyes closed follows the movements of another child. The child who leads must create movement patterns that he can convey to the other child by touch.

1. One child may, for instance, lead another while doing floor patterns. The teacher may give directions: "Each pair of children walk around the room. One child must have his eyes closed and the other child must lead. He should lead only by touching the other child's hand; don't let loose."

A child may learn to change his body position according to the directions given by the leading child. These directions are not verbal; they are always conveyed by a light touch of the hand. A child learns that slight downward pressure on the back of the hand by the other child means to move closer to the floor and a slight upward pull of the hand means to move in a higher position. A slight push can indicate that he should walk backward or forward, and so on. As the children become used to these exercises, the leading child develops movement sequences, while the child with eyes closed becomes bolder, knowing that he is protected and guided.

2. The teacher says, "Now let's try this. If you are the child who is guided, you may move a little on your own, too. Try to be a bit freer. Although you can't see, you can still initiate your own movements. You can indicate to your partner what you want to do and how you want to move. You know you are protected; your partner must not let you bump into anything. Now try. You can move high or low, fast or slow — any way you want to, but you must not let loose of your guide. Your guide may follow you but still protect you. Move as if you were blindfolded. Think about what the guiding child should do and whether he can follow your ideas even though you do not talk."

Creative Movement — 24

Movement in Unison with Eyes Open
This exercise is only for advanced children. Two children stand together, and one child is the leader. They put their hands on each other's shoulders and move any way they want. They may make any floor pattern they choose, but they must try to do it in unison. They may walk, sit down, get up, or dance in a circle, for instance, but they may never lose touch of each other or stop the smooth flow of the movement.

Index

345678974